CLOUD *of* WITNESSES

25 STORIES OF SAINTLY INSPIRATION AND INTERCESSION

WRITE *these* WORDS

CATHOLICITY · CREATIVITY · COMMUNITY

CONTENTS

CONTENTS

FOREWORD

Inside my room in the friary, which we Franciscans often refer to as our cell, I have a rather large crucifix hanging in the center of the wall opposite the window. Next to the crucifix is an icon of the Blessed Virgin Mary. Surrounding Jesus and Mary are icons of some of my dearest friends and greatest teachers. Above the crucifix is an icon of St. John of the Cross, then in clockwise direction, there is an icon of St. Francis of Assisi, St. Anthony of the Desert, St. Bernadette, St. Maximillian Kolbe, St. Catherine of Alexandria, and last but certainly not least, St. John the Baptist.

Every day I spend a few hours in my cell praying, reading, and writing. It is here, gathered with my closest friends and teachers that I "seek the things that are above, where Christ is, seated at the right hand of God" (Colossians 3:1). I would be lying if I said that all or any of these three things are easy. I am, after all, only human and therefore prone to self-absorption, laziness, and confusion. Yet amid my own human difficulties, a simple glance towards one of my friends in the icons not only inspires me and encourages me, but also reminds me that holiness is possible, even for someone like me!

As important as inspiration, encouragement and reminders are, this is not all that my friends do for me. They also teach me, more than any book or class in theology that I have taken has, about God. They teach and show me through their own lives how to love God, how to pray, and perhaps most importantly, how to forget myself so that I can live totally for God alone.

St. John of the Cross has taught me about the complexities and nuances of the spiritual life, while St. Francis of Assisi has revealed to me the riches of poverty. St. Anthony of the Desert has shown me the beauty of solitude, while I have witnessed in the life of St. Bernadette the value of redemptive suffering. St. Maximillian Kolbe has revealed to me the necessity of Mary, the mother of God in my life, while St. Catherine of Alexandria has taught me to be bold and courageous in proclaiming Christ regardless of the cost. Finally, St. John the Baptist has taught me about the prophetic nature of the ascetical life and of the dire necessity that Jesus "must increase, but I must decrease" (John 3:30).

Who then are these mysterious friends that we call saints? The *Catechism of the Catholic Church* defines a saint as "the 'holy one' who leads a life in union with God through the grace of Christ and receives the reward of eternal life" (*CCC* 898). The saints then are those men and women who, despite their sinfulness, brokenness and fears, choose to put all their faith and hope in God and to live only for him. Some of the saints lived very long lives, while others died young. Some of the saints were highly intelligent, while others couldn't even read. Some of the saints were quite busy, proclaiming Christ and serving him in various apostolic endeavors, while others lived in solitude, never traveled and barely spoke to anyone.

Despite these external differences the saints all have one thing in common: A burning love for Jesus Christ and the desire to live only for him. If we truly desire to live as God intends, and hopefully we all do, how can we not love and admire these men and women who have so courageously and generously loved God without limits? Despite what some may believe, honoring the saints and developing a friendship with them is not a hindrance or an obstacle to our relationship with Christ. For it is these dear friends of ours who, through their own life and example, reveal to us more deeply the mystery and beauty of Jesus Christ and show us how to follow him despite our own human limitations. Thus, the saints reveal themselves to us as trustworthy guides and teachers, and those whose friendship we would be wise to cultivate.

My prayer for you then, dear reader, is that as you read the stories of the saints in *Cloud of Witnesses,* you will be reminded of the importance of the saints in your life and that these stories will inspire you with a greater desire to befriend as many of them as possible. By doing so, not only will you find reliable guides and teachers, but friends who will accompany you throughout your life as you journey through this world to heaven.

–Fr. Jeremiah Myriam Shryock CFR
Author of *Amid Passing Things* and *Mary and the Interior Life*
San Juan Diego Friary, Albuquerque, NM
Feast of all the Saints, 2024

INTRODUCTION

"Only God makes saints. Still, it is up to us to tell their stories,"[1] writes Kenneth L. Woodward.

I couldn't agree more.

Indeed, the storyteller in all of us—and we all have one, after all, we are in the image and likeness of an excellent Storyteller–loves to both hear and share incredible stories: narratives of sacrifice, of relentless pursuit, of thrilling reversals, martyrdoms and missions and miracles.

We gravitate toward the stories of those whose lives mirrored that of Jesus Christ–indeed, mysteriously extended it–and yet paradoxically become more of themselves in the process. The saints are men and women gloriously different in temperament, talent, passion, mission, message, time, place and circumstance.

"The simple little girl of Lisieux did not cease to be a Little Flower because she became a Carmelite in the Mystical Body of Christ," Fulton Sheen points out. "Ignatius was a soldier both before and after he became the founder of the Jesuits. Louis IX was a king even though he was subject to the King of Kings ... There is no destruction of nature by grace, but only its elevation to another order."[2]

---

1 Kenneth L. Woodward, *Making Saints: How the Catholic Church Determines Who Becomes a Saint, Who Doesn't and Why* (New York: Simon & Schuster, 1990), 406.
2 Fulton J. Sheen, *In the Fullness of Time: Christ-Centered Wisdom for the Third Millennium* (Liguori, MO: Liguori/Triumph, 1999), 35.

What is more, leaving this earth only reinforced this individuality. We make them "patrons" and call on them for certain help because what they were known for on earth only gets magnified in heaven. Their nature is elevated even further. Need help with technology? Call Carlo Acutis. Struggling to juggle the demands of a household with daily prayer time? Martha wants to help. Finding it hard to finish your writing project? Francis de Sales and Teresa of Avila understand.

So we know of them, and call on them. Sometimes we "discover" them. Sometimes they find their way into our lives in unlikely or surprising ways. We may realize at some point that while we have been allowed to think *we* found and chose our patrons and heavenly friends, they actually knew us first.

The stories in this book reveal that the saints are very much themselves and very much alive. They want to be involved in our lives; they care about what happens to us. They are interested in everything and are always before the throne of God, presenting our needs and desires, and yet at the same time they accompany us closely. "Do not be discouraged. Call me!"[3] St. Elizabeth of the Trinity begged her friends before she died.

I pray that reading these stories (of the saints and of those who love them) will increase your devotion to your favorites and inspire you to befriend others. I hope that the mystery of the communion of saints makes heaven more real, more present, and allows you to live fully in this world while looking forward to the even closer communion to come.

I love these words of Monsignor Charles Pope reflecting on what our communion with each other will look like in heaven:

> As members of one another, we will have deep communion, knowing and being known in a deep and rich way. Your memories, gifts, and insights will be mine, and mine will be yours. There will be profound

---

3   Elizabeth of the Trinity, OCD. *The Complete Works of Elizabeth of the Trinity, Vol. 2: Letters from Carmel.* Translated by Anne Englund Nash (Washington DC: ICS Publications, 2014), 365.

understanding and appreciation, a rich love, and sense of how we all complete one another and are one in Christ.

Imagine the glory of billions of new thoughts, stories, and insights that will come from being perfectly members of Christ and of one another. Imagine the peace that will come from understanding and being understood. This is deep, satisfying, wonderful communion— not crowds of strangers.[4]

This is a cloud of witnesses—a cloud of our closest friends. How blessed are we to run with them!

Since we are surrounded by so great a cloud of witnesses,
let us rid ourselves of every burden and sin that clings to us
and persevere in running the race that lies before us
while keeping our eyes fixed on Jesus,
the leader and perfecter of faith.

Hebrews 12:1

–Claire Dwyer
November 19, 2024
Our Lady of Divine Providence

---

4 Msgr. Charles Pope, "Their Amen: The Feast of All Saints," Spiritual Direction.com, October 2024.

A Hidden Saint

How St. Elizabeth of the Trinity Works
Secretly to Bring Us to God

Claire Dwyer

The chapel in the retreat center was quiet. The women making a silent retreat centered on the life and spirituality of St. Elizabeth of the Trinity had just finished the rosary and were deeply focused in quiet prayer.

From my seat in the back pew, I felt a tap on my shoulder.

"Did you know that there is a relic of St. Elizabeth of the Trinity here? A first-class relic?" The woman behind me, who had earlier introduced herself as someone who came here often, kept her voice to an almost inaudible whisper. I turned to look at her, my eyes wide. Wondering if I had heard her correctly, I shook my head.

She motioned for me to follow her to the front of the small chapel. To the right of the altar was a little alcove with the relics of many saints, and sure enough, among the other heavenly friends, was St. Elizabeth.

I turned to the retreatant. "Did you know this before?"

"No," she mouthed. "I just noticed it."

So there we were, halfway through a retreat on the saint whose relics were just discovered next to the altar in the chapel.

Before I began my talk for the next session, I asked the sixty women in attendance, "How many of you knew we had St. Elizabeth in the chapel?" Only one raised her hand. I explained what we had just realized and suggested they venerate the relic before the retreat ended.

Later that day, I was talking with the retreat center's event coordinator when the chaplain called his cell phone. He answered, and after a few words, turned to me. "Father Kevin wants to know if you can bring your relic of St. Elizabeth of the Trinity to the chapel. The women are asking to venerate it."

I was confused for a moment. "I don't have a relic," I said. "The relic is in the chapel."

He passed the message on to Father Kevin and then turned to me again. "*Our* chapel?" he asked.

I nodded. "In the alcove right off the altar."

"Are you sure?"

"I just saw it," I assured him.

After a few more words with Father Kevin, he hung up and shrugged. "Father had no idea it was there."

The next time I was in the chapel, the relic had a place of honor in the front, with a kneeler where we could pray with our heavenly friend for the rest of the weekend.

I called the chaplain after the retreat to verify that he'd had no idea that St. Elizabeth's relic was among those in the chapel.

Fr. Kevin, who had been with the center for decades, admitted that he did not. "I don't know how she came, who brought her, or when."

I laughed. "It was just like her," I explained. "Elizabeth preferred to be hidden."

St. Elizabeth of the Trinity was born Elizabeth Catez in France in 1880. Like her more famous contemporary, St. Thérèse of Lisieux, she desired to join the cloistered Carmelites at a very young age. However, unlike Therese, Elizabeth encountered strong resistance. Her mother, widowed and with only two girls, couldn't imagine losing one to the convent. She was determined to keep her daughter with her in the world.

Although bitterly disappointed, Elizabeth resigned herself to God's will. She entrusted her vocation to Our Lady and waited patiently for years before her mother finally surrendered and permitted her to enter the Dijon convent in 1901. Becoming a bride of Jesus Christ was her greatest joy and she embraced the austere, hidden life of a Carmelite.

Her letters from the convent reveal what the Lord had taught her in those years of waiting in the world: that intimacy with Him in prayer is not reserved for cloistered nuns. Elizabeth wrote to her mother, sister, and friends, encouraging them to develop and maintain prayer lives in accord with their states in life and to draw near to God even while occupied with their "many things" (Luke 10:41). "Live in His intimacy as you would live with One you love, in a sweet heart-to-heart,"[1] she urged her mother.

She was only in the convent for a few years when she started to experience the symptoms of Addison's Disease, an illness of the adrenal glands that took away her ability to process food and drink.

Elizabeth slowly starved to death over ten months. As her pain intensified, she united her suffering with Jesus and wrote of those excruciating moments, "Believe that at those times he is hollowing out in your soul capacities to receive him, capacities that are, in a way, as infinite as he is himself. Try then to be wholly joyful under the hand that crucifies you."[2]

When she was about to die, her Mother Superior asked if she would return and "come back down" like St. Therese, who had died a few years earlier. Already, the fame of the Little Flower was spreading and the Carmelites in France, including Elizabeth, were well familiar with her promise to "spend her heaven doing good on earth."[3] But Elizabeth declared that she would, instead, shoot "like a rocket" into the bosom of

---

1   Elizabeth of the Trinity, *The Complete Works of Elizabeth of the Trinity, vol. 2. Translated by Anne Englund Nash.* (Washington, DC: Institute of Carmelite Studies, 2014), 113.

2   Ibid., 229.

3   Ibid., 230.

my Three."[4] She had written earlier to her sister, "When the veil is lifted, how happy I will be to disappear into the secret of His Face, and that is where I will spend my eternity, in the bosom of the Trinity that was already my dwelling here below."[5]

True to her word, Elizabeth remained largely unknown in the Church for decades. When St. John Paul II beatified her, he said she had "lived a life hidden with Christ in God." She was not canonized until 2016, over a century after her death, which is not remarkable unless compared to St. Therese, who died in 1899, was beatified in 1923, and canonized in 1925. The rapidity with which her cause went forward was unparalleled in the Church. Everyone knew the Little Flower.

But Elizabeth stayed hidden.

She stayed hidden through world wars and Church councils, dark times and revivals, schisms and renewals. She stayed hidden while the Church suffered, was scandalized, and stayed faithful. She stayed hidden while souls learned to love—learned to love through waiting and suffering.

Finally, she began to emerge as an intercessor and a teacher of prayer. And we realized, somehow, that she had always been with us. We had good reason for suspecting so. Before she died, Elizabeth relented a little. "I think in heaven," she said, "my mission will be to draw souls by helping them go out of themselves to cling to God by a wholly simple and loving movement, and to keep them in this great silence, which will allow God to communicate Himself to them and transform them into Himself."[6]

In other words, while hidden, Elizabeth would be working—but she would be secretly working to draw us to God. And the sign that she had been praying for us would not be outward miracles. It would be a new depth to our prayer. An interior stillness. A capacity for love and suffering. She would slip in silently and gently bring us before God, into the same

---

4 Joanne Mosley, *Elizabeth of the Trinity: The Unfolding of Her Message*, vol 2. (Oxford: Teresian Press, 2012), 194.

5 Complete Works, vol. 2, 264.

6 Ibid., 360.

hiding place she had found. And when we found ourselves closer to Him, we'd know—she had been with us.

Elizabeth also liked to hide things to be found.

While in the final stages of her illness, in her agony, she wrote a letter to her Mother Superior and dear friend, Mother Germaine. She hid it away for Mother Germaine to find after her death. This letter, now known as "Let Yourself Be Loved" is considered one of her major works and was a direct and tender appeal. She urged her friend to consider her vocation to "be loved."

"If you faithfully believe that He is still working, that He is loving you just the same, and even more: because His love is free and that is how He wants to be magnified in you, and you will let yourself be loved."[7] No less than six times she would repeat "Let yourself be loved" in that single letter, In an age when we have awakened to the great need for healing—as a Church and as individuals—Elizabeth reveals to us that letting God love us is necessary not just for our holiness, but *our wholeness*.

But how do we do that, exactly?

Elizabeth would remind us that drawing near to Him in prayer—even while living busy, increasingly noisy lives—is the way. Our life in the world does not preclude Him from doing the deep, often hidden work of healing. Maybe it had to be a hidden saint to show us the lost places within us, places waiting to be loved.

I have always smiled at the memory of the retreat center story. She seemed to be saying in her hiddenness, "Never mind me; just look at Jesus." The Church loves to make introductions and bring friends together. It was time.

Come out Elizabeth, and show them who has been praying for them all along.

---

7   Elizabeth of the Trinity, *Complete Works*, vol. 1. Translated by Sister Aletheia Kane, OCD (Washington, DC, Institute of Carmelite Studies, 2014), 180.

The following litany, the "*Be Loved Litany*," can be recited as we pray to be able to receive the love of God like His hidden saint.

St. Elizabeth of the Trinity, pray for us.

As a child of God, known and knit together in my mother's womb
Lord, let me believe in your love.

As a child of God, baptized to be a dwelling place of the Holy Trinity
Lord, let me believe in your love.

As a child of God, rescued, redeemed, and recreated
Lord, let me believe in your love.

As a child of God, chosen and anointed for a purpose
Lord, let me believe in your love.

When I am swallowed up in self-condemnation
Lord, let me receive your love.

When I am tempted to hopelessness and quiet despair
Lord, let me receive your love.

When I am experiencing the ache of longing and loneliness
Lord, let me receive your love.

When I am overwhelmed by the demands of life
Lord, let me receive your love.

In the place of my deepest wounds
Lord, love me there.

In the place of my secret shame
Lord, love me there.

In the place of my buried memories
Lord, love me there.

In the place of the enemy's strongholds
Lord, love me there.

With bold confidence
Let me rejoice in your love, Lord.

With childlike faith
Let me rejoice in your love, Lord.

With reverent awe
Let me rejoice in your love, Lord.

With profound gratitude
Let me rejoice in your love, Lord.

That others may be consoled
Let me reveal your love, Lord.

That others may be healed
Let me reveal your love, Lord.

That others may be strengthened
Let me reveal your love, Lord.

That others may be given a future and a hope
Let me reveal your love, Lord.

Through intimacy with you in prayer
Open my heart even more to your love, Lord.

Through the grace of the sacraments
Open my heart even more to your love, Lord.

Through the sweetness of suffering with you
Open my heart even more to your love, Lord.

Through the continuous revelation of Yourself in this present paradise
Open my heart even more to your love, Lord.

Father, Author of my life,
 I love you.

Jesus, Redeemer of my life,
I love you.

Holy Spirit, Sanctifier of my life,
 I love you.

Holy Mary, whose maternal mission is to lead me deeper into the love of the Trinity,
Pray for me.

Amen.

Claire Dwyer writes with a desire that all know how deeply they are loved by God. Speaker, retreat leader, and author of *This Present Paradise: A Spiritual Journey with St. Elizabeth of the Trinity*, she loves leading others into friendship with the saints. Find out more—and download your printable copy of the *"Be Loved Litany"*—at *clairedwyer.com*.

II

Sometimes Lost, Always Found

How St. Anthony Helped Me
Find More Than What Was Lost

Mike Fontecchio

On my way back from making what I thought was the last payment
to our contractor for a major addition to our home, my phone rang.

"Mike," the contractor said. "I'm not sure who you sent that wire
transfer to, but you need to call your bank right away. That's not my
account number."

I had no idea that the email I had received earlier that day was not
really from my contractor. Upon closer look, it appeared identical, with
the name and address matching that of my contractor. Only it wasn't him.

Over $8,000 had just been stolen from us.

I couldn't help but think of Uncle Billy who had lost the same sum
of money in *It's a Wonderful Life*, one of my family's favorite Christmas
movies. Thoughts began to race through my head. *Wasn't I supposed to
be the caretaker of our family's funds? How could this happen to* **me**? The
hard truth became clear—the money had left the account. It was gone.

We were at the end of the ten-week project, which was already over
budget. I was eager to see everything completed and was ready to be done
making payments. The thief had likely been studying our email exchanges

and waited for the right time to make a move, like the enemy, always lurking, waiting to strike when we are vulnerable, unsuspecting, and our guard is down.

I called my wife to let her know what happened. She leaned into this painful struggle with me and immediately suggested we give the situation entirely to prayer. I knew my beloved confirmation saint, Anthony of Padua, agreed.

As a child, I had taken an interest in St. Anthony because his June 13 feast day was a few days after my birthday. I had also often heard my mom praying to him to help find the keys to the car. Who hasn't prayed to St. Anthony for that?

The more I prayed about what to do, I started to wonder if Anthony was seeking me out after all these years. What was this humble preacher, a wonder-worker, trying to teach me?

St. Anthony, born Fernando Martins de Bulhões in Lisbon, Portugal, in 1195, was son to a prominent family in the region. He entered religious formation at the age of fifteen, and after nine years of study as an Augustinian friar, had a profound experience with a group of five Franciscan priests he had befriended. Those Franciscans had been preparing to preach the faith in Morocco to the Moors, knowing their martyrdom was imminent.

Five months later, those five friars were beheaded and a burial ceremony was held in the town where their remains were carried in a solemn procession to the same monastery where Fernando lived. Fernando was so moved that he soon requested to join the Franciscan order, under the condition that he would be allowed to preach the Gospel in Morocco. At the age of twenty-six, he was permitted to leave the Augustinians to become a Franciscan, taking the name Anthony, where he immediately set out for Morocco.

As providence would have it, while in Morocco, Anthony became seriously ill, and after several months, he knew he needed to return home.

God's will for Anthony was not that he become a martyr preaching to the Moors, but something more.

On the journey home, his ship blew off course and he ended up in Sicily, where he was nurtured back to health by a group of Franciscans. During his time there, Anthony longed to meet his contemporary, St. Francis of Assisi, born just thirteen years before St. Anthony.

Anthony was later transferred to the order in Assisi, where he remained largely unknown. He was responsible for less important tasks, such as washing the dishes and greeting guests. Anthony performed his duties humbly and with a servant's heart.

During an ordination ceremony where both Franciscans and Dominicans were present, it was customary for a Dominican to preach for the occasion. The assigned Dominican preacher was unable to make it in time, so Anthony was called upon to say "something simple." After his initial refusal, Anthony leaned in to this request and began to preach with passion and conviction. The bright light that burned within Anthony shone for all to see and hear.

The world had found St. Anthony.

Reports were made to St. Francis of Anthony's sermons, his preaching of Scripture, and his devotion to Our Lady. This all led to Anthony becoming the first teacher of the Franciscan order to be given special approval and the blessings of St. Francis. In his letter to Anthony, he wrote, "It pleases me that you should teach the friars sacred theology, provided that in such studies they do not destroy the spirit of holy prayer and devotedness, as contained in the Rule."[1]

As a Franciscan friar, Anthony vowed to live his vows of poverty, chastity, and obedience. He remained humble, frequently sought solitude to pray, and actively chose to live his vocation among the people. He began to attract crowds whenever he spoke, sometimes in excess of 30,000. The churches could not hold the crowds, so Anthony preached in the piazzas

---

1   https://www.stanthony.org/who-st-anthony

or open fields where people would wait all night to hear him. After morning Mass, often Anthony would spend the day hearing confessions.

Anthony, considered the "greatest son of St. Francis," preached to the unbelievers of his time about the goodness of God. He believed the purpose of his teaching was not to prove people wrong, but to try to win lost souls to the faith through presenting the Truth in love. After hearing Anthony preach, many people would experience true sorrow for their sins, which led them to repentance, and ultimately to a deeper reconciliation with their loving Father.

While Anthony is referred to as the "'hammer of the heretics," he was said to have never engaged in dialogue in a combative way. He was admired because he lived his life as a witness to the Faith. He was truly following the Rule of St. Francis and the Gospel message: "Children, let us love not in word or speech but in deed and truth" (1 John 3:18).

On one occasion, a novitiate who had left the Franciscan order was said to have stolen Anthony's treasured Psalter book, which contained many of his notes and personal reflections. Anthony prayed fervently for *both* the return of his prayer book *and* the conversion of the novitiate. The novitiate would later return Anthony's prayer book and repent of his actions. He was also allowed to rejoin the order.

Anthony was well on his way to helping others find God.

Likewise, I was turning more towards my need for God's guidance and to my confirmation saint, St. Anthony, for his intercession in finding the lost funds.

I had already gone through all the proper legal channels. I had filed a claim, contacted the authorities, and made multiple phone calls to the bank. Each time I called, I was told, "We are working on it." It was a dead end.

I gradually realized I had to let go of the funds and rely more on God. Not only did I need to learn how to cope with this present loss, but ultimately, I needed to completely entrust all of our finances to the Lord and let Him lead.

*But having something stolen from us is unjust, Lord. How do I **let that go**?*

I still had to work through feelings of resentment towards whomever did this. ***Why** did they do this to us*?

In prayer one morning, a clear sign came from Psalm 37:5–7:

> Commit your way to the Lord; trust in him, and he will act. He will bring forth your vindication as the light, and your right like the noonday. Be still before the Lord, and wait patiently for him; do not fret over him who prospers in his way, over the man who carries out evil devices!

A peace immediately came upon me, and I felt the Lord's gentle words "I got this" fill my spirit. The Scripture verse and words of consolation were everything I needed and more.

I meditated more deeply on this verse. How could I "be still before the Lord and wait for him"? After all, questions were still circling in my head. *How is this going to be resolved, Lord? Will I wake up tomorrow and see that the money was returned to the account? Will the bank call to let me know it's been taken care of? Will a check come in the mail?*

Weeks went by and I heard nothing, but the peace remained. I could do no more than to keep waiting, praying, hoping, and trusting in the Lord.

Week after week, it became clear that this was no longer about "getting back" what was taken from me. Anthony, my dear friend in heaven, was busy helping me find God in a deeper way *again*.

Anthony loved the poor and Our Lady, and was inviting me to do more of both.

I began to look at our tithing. *Where can I give more of my time, treasure, and talents? And how can I draw closer to Our Lady, the Undoer of Knots?* I renewed my consecration to Mary, and decided to commit myself to a concerted effort to pray the Rosary daily.

I also reflected upon a time years ago where I made the decision to leave a job and needed to trust the Lord fully. I learned during that time that that God *always* provides, and He is always *for* us. I knew in that moment He wasn't going to stop caring for me or my family. I needed not be anxious about anything, especially money.

+ + +

In the month that followed, I began to see a surge in my business. A new project idea took off. Long-time clients reached out asking for more help. Three new projects in three days. Business-wise, I experienced my best month ever, thanks be to God.

Anthony didn't just want me to recover something that was stolen; he was interceding for me to find a deeper relationship with our Lord, built on trust, confidence, and a deeper surrendering of all to Him. I was learning that the more we give to the Lord, the more He can multiply our efforts.

To this day, those funds have not been returned. It's OK, because for me, it's no longer about the money. Anthony didn't want me to limit my thinking to just "getting back what I thought belonged to me." He was leading me deeper, into something more lasting and eternal. He was also helping me find peace.

Years ago, my mother had obtained a small relic of St. Anthony that included the following prayer:

St. Anthony, help me experience peace of mind and heart in my present needs (here mention). Free me from needless worry and burdensome fears. Grant me unfailing trust and an awareness of God's loving mercy. Amen.

I also came upon this prayer to St. Anthony for those facing financial difficulties:

O holy St. Anthony, you often expressed loving concern for the poor and needy, and you worked miracles to relieve their suffering. Please come to my assistance when I or my loved ones experience financial problems. At this time I especially place in your care these financial worries (here mention) which are troubling to me or those I love.

Teach all of us not to be desirous of wealth and possessions, but instead give us generous hearts to share what we have with those less fortunate. Amen.[2]

Thank you, St. Anthony for helping me find more than what I ask for, more of what I need.

Mike Fontecchio has worked as a graphic designer in Catholic publishing for nearly thirty years and provides publishing services through his company, Faith & Family Publications. He is husband to Amy and father to six children. Mike and his family live outside of Philadelphia, where he loves coaching youth sports. Find out more at *faithandfamilypublications.com*.

---

2   St. Anthony of Padua Prayer Book, *Companions of St. Anthony,* 29.

III

WOMB TO TOMB

How St. Teresa of Calcutta Taught Me to Care for the Most Vulnerable

Beth Casteel

James lies flat in the nursing home bed, partially covered by a white sheet. He is naked except for an adult diaper. His thick silver hair is brushed away from his face. Even though he has been a patient here for at least ten years, he has no decorations in his room—nothing to indicate that he belongs to someone. His radio plays Electric Light Orchestra's "Evil Woman" inches from his head. I gently shake him awake. "James, do you want Holy Communion?" He squints through one eye at me. His bearded Baptist roommate yells from behind the curtain that separates them, "James, get up and take Communion."

James doesn't sit up, but he answers, "Yes," and nods his head.

I hold up the Sacred Host between us, make the Sign of the Cross, and say, "Behold the Lamb of God." He repeats every word I say. "Lord, I am not worthy that you should enter under my roof ... " He moves the host around in his mouth. Thirst, parched lips, a desire for the most basic needs to be satiated, especially a desire to be seen, loved, touched, are universal in this anteroom to death.

I rub his arm and ask if he needs water.

After this Jesus, knowing that all was now finished, said (to fulfill the scripture), "I thirst." A bowl full of vinegar stood there; so they put a sponge full of the vinegar on hyssop and held it to his mouth. When Jesus had received the vinegar, he said, "It is finished"; and he bowed his head and gave up his spirit (John 19:28–30).

St. Teresa of Calcutta had "I Thirst" painted next to the crucifixes that hang in every Missionaries of Charity chapel. "We have these words in every chapel of the MCs to remind us what an MC is here for: to quench the thirst of Jesus for souls, for love, for kindness, for compassion, for delicate love,"[1] she explained. Mother Teresa saw the Lord's thirst in the poorest of the poor, and she also saw it in the spiritual poverty of those in first world countries. "The greatest disease in the West today is not TB or leprosy; it is being unwanted, unloved, and uncared for," she said.[2]

This nursing home in rural southwestern Pennsylvania, where I go to take communion with a friend, sits far from Mother Teresa's homes for the dying destitute in Calcutta, India, but its symptoms are the same. The loneliness is acute. The suffering is purgation. The halls are filled with the smell of bodies in decay, the sorrowful cries of those who are in pain, and the tired faces of the caregivers.

Mother Teresa told her sisters to do everything with a smile, but I struggle to smile for the two hours we are there. I often struggle to smile in my domestic caregiving role as a daughter, a wife, a mother, and a grandmother. "Seeking the face of God in everything, everyone, all the time, and his hand in every happening; this is what it means to be contemplative in the heart of the world," Mother Teresa said.[3]

St. Teresa of Calcutta was born August 26, 1910 as Anjezë (Agnes) Gonxha Bojaxhiu in Skopje—then the Ottoman Empire but now known as Northern Macedonia—to Albanian parents, Nikollë and Dranafile

1 Brian Kolodiejchuk, *Where there is Love, There is God*,(New York: Doubleday, 2010), 51.
2 Mother Teresa, compiled by Lucinda Vardey, *A Simple Path*,(New York: Ballantine Books, 1995), 79.
3 Mother Teresa, *In the Heart of the World*, (California: New World Library, 2010), 10.

Bojaxhiu. She was the youngest of three children. Gonxha, a Turkish name meaning rosebud, was baptized one day after her birth and received first Holy Communion at age seven at the Sacred Heart of Jesus Catholic Church in Skopje. In this same church, she played the mandolin, sang in the choir, acted in theatrical productions, danced, recited, and wrote poetry.

Family life was comfortable, loving, and devoutly Catholic. Nikollë and Dranafile gave generously to the poor. When Agnes was only eight or nine, her father, Nikollë, a philanthropist, businessman, and a politician, died suddenly. He was believed to have been poisoned because of his opinion in favor of uniting the Albanian territory.[4] His death created financial struggles, but Dranafile continued to do all she could to help those in need.

Agnes began to feel pulled to the Lord's service at age twelve when Jesuit priests spoke to her youth group about missionary work in India and Africa. On September 26, 1928, at the age of eighteen, she responded to that call and joined the Sisters of Loreto in Dublin, Ireland. She never saw her mother or her sister again, even though she petitioned the communist government for twenty years to do so.

Agnes spent two months of intensive training with the sisters in Dublin, including learning English. She left Ireland on December 1, 1928, and arrived in Calcutta on the feast of Epiphany, January 6, 1929. Religious formation continued in Darjeeling, which sits at the foothills of the Himalayas, four hundred miles from Calcutta. Agnes made her first profession of vows on May 25, 1931, taking the religious name Teresa in honor of St. Thérèse of Lisieux and was assigned to the Loreto community in Calcutta as a teacher at St. Mary's Bengali Medium School for girls. Following Loreto custom, she took the name "Mother" after her final vows occurred on May 24, 1937, in the Darjeeling convent chapel.

---

4   Anne Sebba, *Mother Teresa, Beyond the Image* (New York: Doubleday Religion, 1997). First chapter published in the *New York Times*.

Mother Teresa served the girls at St. Mary's with great love and had no intention of leaving until she received the "call within a call," September 1946, while on a train to a retreat at the Loreto Convent in Darjeeling. "It was in that train; I heard the call to give up all and follow Him into the slums—to serve Him in the poorest of the poor." Mother called this the real beginning of the Missionaries of Charity.[5] Over the ensuing weeks and months, Jesus continued to reveal his desire for her to serve the poor and to found a religious group of sisters to help her.

She struggled with leaving the Sisters of Our Lady of Loreto.

> I had received my spiritual formation, become a nun and consecrated my life to God in the Congregation of Our Lady of Loreto. I loved the work to which the congregation had assigned me at St. Mary's High School in Calcutta. For this reason, I paid a tremendous price by taking the step of leaving forever what had become my second family. When I closed the door of the convent behind me on Aug. 16, 1948, and found myself alone on the streets of Calcutta, I experienced a strong feeling of loss and almost of fear that was difficult to overcome.[6]

She traded her religious habit for the white and blue sari that unified her with the poorest women in India and the Blessed Virgin Mary, took a crash course in nursing, and acquired lifelong Indian citizenship to prepare herself for the grueling work of serving the street poor. On October 7, 1950, Mother Teresa received papal permission to start the Missionaries of Charity order. The facts of her life seem orderly and deliberate, but the separation from her family, and then the loving environment provided by the Loreto sisters, was grueling for her. Worldwide recognition of her work with the poor overshadowed the seventeen years that she spent teaching and the difficult decision she made to step out of the comfort

---

5   Mother Teresa, edited with commentary by Brian Kolodiejchuk, M.C., *Come Be My Light* (New York: Doubleday, 2007), 40.

6   Renzo Allegri, taken from *New Covenant Magazine*, 1996, ewtn.com.

of the convent school and into the slums, where she immediately began living alongside the poor.

The television introduced me to Mother in the 1970s and '80s—images of her stooping to care for emaciated men in metal cots and scooping her arms around infants in her orphanages. I remember watching Princess Diana bending down to hold her wrinkled hands. I was fascinated by this living saint who touched the open sores of the poor and the bejeweled hands of a princess. Her face graced the front of a 1975 issue of Time magazine. And 1979 news accounts broadcast her acceptance speech for the Nobel Peace Prize. She spoke of the importance of accepting and caring for children.

> We have brought so much joy in the homes that there was not a child, and so today, I ask His Majesties here before you all who come from different countries, let us all pray that we have the courage to stand by the unborn child, and give the child an opportunity to love and to be loved, and I think with God's grace we will be able to bring peace in the world. [7]

I reflected on her example years later as my husband and I stumbled through infertility and when my parish priest directed us to Catholic Charities to pursue adoption. I prayed for the intercession of Mother Teresa. I listened to her words, I begged for her direction, and I observed her actions as we adopted our first infant, a daughter, in the United States in 1994 and then three more babies in Guatemala—a daughter in 1998, a son in 2002, and our third daughter in 2003. We experienced vulnerability in the heart pain of their birthmothers, in the ripping away at the fabric of our children's genealogy and culture, and in our own expectations of parenting. Jesus placed the call to adopt on my heart. Mother Teresa held my hand and walked me there.

After her death on September 5, 1997, I bought my first book authored by her. I found it in the piles of dusty secondhand books at a discount store. The large-print paperback version of *No Greater Love* cost me $2.99.

---

7   Nobelprize.org, *The Nobel Peace Prize 1979, Mother Teresa Acceptance Speech.*

At the moment of our death, you and I, whoever we might have been and wherever we have lived, Christians and non-Christians alike, every human being who has been created by the loving hand of God in His own image, shall stand in His presence and be judged according to what we have been for the poor. [8]

My collection of writings about Mother Teresa now fills a bookshelf. *Come Be My Light* most profoundly punctuated my path. "I want to smile at Jesus and so hide if possible, the pain and the darkness of my soul even from Him," said Mother.[9] Her spiritual darkness, which was not revealed until after her death, gave me reason for perseverance in times of great trial. Through her, I began to understand prayer despite consolations and in periods of doubt and despair. Reading her private journal entries created intimacy for me in my own conversations with God. I clung to her silent suffering and attached it to my own. "That terrible longing keeps growing—& I feel as if something will break in me one day—and then that darkness, that loneliness, that feeling of terrible aloneness. Heaven from every side is closed … and yet—I long for God. I long to love Him with every drop of life in me—and I want to love Him with a deep personal love," said this saint who suffered in spiritual darkness for fifty years.[10]

I have made Mother Teresa my patron saint, even though I don't share her name. She was born on my wedding day—August 26—and she arrived in Calcutta on my birthday—January 6.

I have rosary bracelets, prayer cards, and a coffee mug with the quote "I can cast a stone that creates many ripples" that sits nearby as I write. I have watched documentaries and listened to audiobooks about her, marveling at the fact that I can hear the voice of a saint. Her message continues to move me profoundly.

---

8 Mother Teresa, *No Greater Love,* (New York: Walker and Company, 1997), 101.

9 Mother Teresa, *Come Be My Light,* 149.

10 Ibid., 202–203.

Until the year she died, Mother spoke of satiating the thirst of Jesus. "The more we understand this thirst of Jesus, the more united and the closer we come to Jesus because it is the tremendous thirst of Jesus's heart... Just think, God is thirsting for you and me to come forward to satiate his thirst. Just think of that."[11]

I think of it every time I gaze upon the crucifix, but I am too often handing bitter sorrow back to Jesus. Recognizing Him in every person is hard. I can only pray that Mother's words drip into my discontent and direct me to dig deeper into the spring of eternal water that quenches divine thirst.

In 2012, on a family trip to Rome, I spent some time praying at the tomb of St. John Paul II and was overwhelmed by the presence of the Holy Spirit. The pope and Mother Teresa had a deep respect for one another, and it was the aging pope who fast tracked her cause toward canonization, which transpired on September 4, 2016, by Pope Francis. Both saints gave us a public view of aging with dignity. Some questioned why St. John Paul II moved her case along so quickly, but I think in honoring her role as Mother to the vulnerable he validated the caregiver in all of us.

In the nursing home, it is hard to secure a minute of quiet contemplation. Televisions blare news reports, *Golden Girls,* and *Gunsmoke.* A staff member cleans the bathroom while another is running a floor cleaning machine in the hallway; a cafeteria worker is delivering lunch trays and a nurse is waiting to take vitals. James closes his eyes as he swallows the sacred host. "Thank you," he utters as he slips back to sleep. The roommate waves and says, "God bless you. Thank you."

I feel guilty about how little time we have spent with these two men, but Robert is just down the hall, and he will be waiting for us.

---

11 Ibid., 160.

Beth A. Casteel searches for truth in the messiness of life. She worked as a journalist and earned an MFA in creative nonfiction from Carlow University, but her greatest calling has been to motherhood. Beth has been an organist for nearly forty years and has served in women's ministry. You can interact with her at *bethcasteel.com*.

IV

INTO THE WILDERNESS

How St. Antony of the Desert Helped Me Embrace Simplicity and Detachment

Natalie Hanemann

A rriving at the Eye of the Sandias trailhead, a four-mile trail near Albuquerque, New Mexico, I picked a blue juniper berry off a nearby evergreen and cracked it open with my thumbnail. The scent of pine infused the air, and I smiled. I couldn't believe it; I was actually standing in a desert. The temperature would increase by thirty degrees as the sun ascended over the next six hours, typical for July in New Mexico, but the sixty-degree air felt crisp and unpolluted.

I adjusted my visor and started walking, in awe of so much flat, open space. The hills and rocky land of my hometown in Tennessee offered a diversity of views, but none so uncluttered. At home, rolling pasturelands dotted with Black Angus and forests of Eastern red cedar created the backdrop. The New Mexico desert, however, didn't match the one I had created in my imagination. It wasn't a wasteland of loose, fine-grained, blonde sand with dune after dune extending to the horizon line, where a mirage of palm trees and a watering hole manifested in the distance. Instead, as I gazed at the scene, I noticed tube-stemmed cholla cacti, knee-high dried grass patches, and a spattering of dwarfed trees were all that interrupted the view from earth to sky, with the distant monolith of rocky red mountains that were the Sandias—Spanish for "watermelon," because of the rose-colored hue of the rocks at dawn and dusk.

At home, I had come to rely on the natural world to calm my restlessness, but standing here, on this sandy, graveled dirt path, the environment gave me a different feeling—one of absolute freedom.

St. Antony, is this how you felt?

+ + +

During the summer of 2022, COVID restrictions had finally begun loosening, and I was close to completing my graduate degree in theology. Sheltering in place had allowed me just enough hours in the day to plow through the substantial reading material for my Church history class.

What I could not have known then, but see now with the clarity of hindsight, is how St. Antony was the catalyst for ground-shifting changes in my spiritual life, my professional life, and my physical health.

+ + +

We are fortunate that another saint, Athanasius, felt so inspired by Antony, who was his friend and contemporary, that he wrote a biography of the Egyptian. From *The Life of Saint Antony*, we learn how, at age nineteen, the newly orphaned Antony attended church and heard Matthew 19:21. Jesus said to [the rich young ruler], "If you would be perfect, go, sell what you possess and give to the poor, and you will have treasure in heaven; and come, follow me."

The young ruler walked away, unable or unwilling to let go of the material goods he'd amassed.

Jesus explained to the apostles how hard it will be for a wealthy person to enter the kingdom of God. So hard, it would be easier for a camel to pass through the eye of a needle (Matthew 19:24). Jesus was making it known what God's expectation was for those who choose to follow Him:

If asked, we must be willing to give away all we have, even our very life. True discipleship requires detaching from that which distracts us from intimacy with God.

Inspired by Jesus's words, Antony arranged for his younger sister's care at the nearby convent, promptly sold off his wealthy family's possessions, and gave the proceeds to the poor.

I set down the reading and looked around my room, crowded with more possessions than I could ever possibly need. I imagined myself in Antony's shoes. He so desired the kingdom of God, he was willing to forsake everything to attain it. Was I willing to let the Gospel inspire me to have such a radical response?

Surprising myself, I rather enjoyed the thought of following Antony's example. I was entering midlife and felt crowded by the stacks of plastic containers that held the school projects from my four kids, a closetful of clothes that no longer fit me, and stacks of old electric bills and junk mail. Drawers of unused items: puzzles with missing pieces, boxes of old books we would never read again, socks with holes, buried receipts for items we no longer owned. The house wasn't too small; our possessions were crowding us out!

I realized the container that held the details of the family my husband and I had curated had reached full capacity. Practically speaking, I could choose to sort through it all and label piles "keep," "trash," and "donate," but lacing up my tennies and walking outside seemed much easier. Maybe I'm the only one who watched the movie *Forrest Gump* and felt envious when Forrest left his Alabama plantation with just his running shoes on and kept going, day after day, until he reached one coastline, then turned around and ran till he hit the other coastline. Hiking alone, up along the Sandia Mountains, across a huge expanse of wide-open space, made me feel the same kind of freedom—a healthy detachment from all the items I had accumulated and a diminishing desire to keep holding on to unnecessary possessions.

How long would I keep the baby blankets I had swaddled my children in? Frayed and loved thin, what purpose did they serve anymore? Yet, discarding them, items I considered sacred, felt wrong. Could I hold those precious items only inside my mind? My memory of the pattern or the texture of the fabric may fade, but that would happen either way. Would there come a day when I would search frantically through boxes and bins, looking for those blankets so I could relive the tender sweet years of their infancies?

After returning home from Albuquerque, I printed the photos I took on my hike and grimaced. The distances looked compressed, the depths flattened. They in no way captured the volume of space.

In a similar way, was I trying to capture a moment in time that defied description?

Was I desperately trying to hold onto the sweet and tender years when my children were little and life was much simpler? Like my view of the land and sky out west, do the souvenirs or keepsakes really help me hold on to the value of my experience? Those moments pass and then no longer exist, in the same way a river is never the same because different water is constantly flowing. It isn't the blanket that is so precious, it's the girl who dragged it around, sleepy and safe, trusting and innocent.

Antony walked into the wilderness with few provisions, and he battled the environment. He also battled the demons who relentlessly tormented him. He battled himself, fighting not to let his body rule his mind, but instead remain properly ordered: body to mind to spirit to God. I wanted that kind of order.

I hopped up and went to my husband. "Hey, would you be OK if Mae and I take a trip out West? I want to see a desert."

My eleven-year-old daughter and I had been taking annual "mother–daughter trips." We had gone to places within driving distance, such as Gatlinburg, Tennessee, and Boone, North Carolina, where I had gone to college. With COVID grounding us from normal life, and with the threat slowly waning, I decided it was as good a time as ever to take an adventure. For my daughter, as long as it wasn't the ocean and didn't involve too much physical exertion, she was game. I booked two tickets before I could change my mind.

Making an impulsive decision to fly across the country, to a place I had never been, was new behavior for me. I had always been more likely to stay at home, read, and avoid large crowds, but something new stirred in me. The streak of gray blooming at my temples, stark against my dark hair, was growing more apparent. I've never felt the urge to fight aging. I don't mind the fanned out lines around my eyes and the skin of my neck loosening. However, what I would fight to preserve was this precious and lessening time I had with two good knees, a sharp mind, and a curiosity about places and people. What I decidedly would not do is keep walking in circles on the sidewalks of my neighborhood and only reading about other people's adventures.

When Antony walked away from his village, located south of present-day Cairo, he had no idea the grit and determination that would be required of him to survive in such a harsh environment. The land siphoned away all moisture, leaving dried-out carcasses that would eventually be buried by the wind and sand. When first setting out, he traveled to see other monks in the region who were successfully living as hermits and became their student. Antony began a lifelong study of detachment.

I couldn't help but feel like I wasn't alone on the 2.4-mile trail hike up to the ridgeline, around the saddle, then back down, though I saw no other hikers. The solitude amplified the intensity of the rugged terrain and sent my imagination to wonder about wild animals and how I would find help if I injured myself. Of course, I had no cell reception on the more remote sections of the trail, but I reminded myself, St. Antony hadn't even had a phone.

Hikers sometimes experience a phenomenon called Trail Panic, in which they become disoriented and panicky when out in the wilderness, and I experienced it during this hike. I didn't remember the exact length of the trail, so I didn't know how much farther I had to go, which seriously disoriented me. Only one thing settled me … I began to sing a Hail Mary over and over. After daily Mass at my parish, the congregation sang the Hail Mary and then recited the St. Michael prayer. These prayers felt like a blanket thrown over me, warm and comforting.

I thought of St. Antony and how he may have felt in those first days out in the open, alone in the unfamiliar. *Could he look down and see me out here?*

So much freedom all at once can often feel like being under a microscope of the great eye in the sky. The truth was, though, God was looking down on me, as was the namesake of this trail—the Eye of the Sandia, which had been painted on a boulder of this trail in the sixties. Even the mule deer and elk observed me, the crazy singing lady, but I kept moving. Then, spying the trailhead sign, I shifted into a run and finished strong.

This hike was the start of a radical metanoia concerning my progressive detachment and my relationship with the outdoors. I began to spend more time in remote wilderness. I got an unexpected hiking companion: Jesus. Turns out He likes the outdoors a lot too.

My hikes became prayer.

I also slowly started weeding through the clutter at home and simplifying. I got a rain barrel to water my garden and hung a clothesline, so I ran the dryer less. I started writing about how God was meeting me on the trail. In 2024, I expanded my writing and editing business to include a wilderness component and hope to begin wilderness writing retreats in the near future.

I shudder to think how easily I could have missed reading about the desert saint in that chapter about the birth of monasticism. Who would I be today, years later, had I rushed through or skipped that chapter? I always knew my vocation was to marriage and motherhood, but I never expected to have a second calling that would take me to the outreaches of the natural world to meet the eternal, unbound, merciful love of God. Thank you, St. Antony.

+ + +

St. Antony, you left the comfort of the world and settled in the inhospitable desert. There, silence and solitude helped you grow deeper in communion with God. Pray for me, beloved saint, that I model your discipline and continue to prioritize the deep desire I have to spend time alone with God in the beauty of the natural world.

Natalie Hanemann is a contributing writer for CatholicMom.com and CatholicStand.com. She began taking solo adventures in the remote outdoors to test her limits and make friends with the critic inside her. What she discovered was a deeper understanding of herself and the abundant grace of God. Read more about Natalie by visiting *youbewilder.com*

V

A LOVING GOD

How Venerable Fulton Sheen Helped Me Find Peace of Soul

Helen Syski

Rise my breast!
But iron ribs compress
like coils of a serpent
                -till spent-
the heart's thready pound
                and blood rush
                        ends in hush.
How am I alive
        with such terror-
How do my lungs breathe-
though no air comes-
How does my heart beat-
though my blood is stopped?[1]

A shadowy demon had hounded me for years. I knew he was there, lurking amongst my prayers and devotions. In my peripheral vision

---

1   Original poem by Helen Syski.

I could see him move, flitting in the shadows from one teaching of the Church to another ... until I focused on him and thought I had pinned him under my thumb, then he was gone.

My husband and I had been receiving formation by a Catholic group for years. The words were the teaching of the Church, but something was off—something that was strangling our supernatural and natural life. The stacks of pious practices crushed the tender bud of our young family; the spiritual direction seeded mistrust between my husband and me. Yet nothing was against the Magisterium. We were giving everything to God. We were told we were on dry land, while the waves of life were washing over our heads and the group's riptide threatened to carry my husband away from me.

In a final cry for breath, we withdrew from the group and plunged into our interior mess. We chose to trust that God was there, speaking to us in our turmoil. We clung to our wedding vows and their sacramental grace as the life raft that could save us from our shipwreck.

Together we sought the loving Father I had known as a child: A God whose love is always there, never earned. A God who has Ten Commandments instead of a thousand. A God who is found in our breathing, our eating, our play, our work. A God whose graces flow because we are exactly where He has placed us: in family life.

After that decision, joy slowly reentered our family. Our marriage healed with a new depth of love and commitment. Still, it was hard to shake the demon whose voice was so well known to us but we couldn't name. He breathed on the words spoken to us in homilies, in spiritual articles, in the voices of people around us. The demon's doubt ate at our peace. When we stayed close to each other, listening to God, trusting in His love, responding with gratitude to His fruits, we found peace and even bliss permeating our family life, but just a word could sunder our new road and anxiety would descend in a deluge once more.

One day I found in my hands a book by Fulton Sheen, *Peace of Soul*. I had always loved Fulton Sheen for his incredible mind. The clarity with which he grasped the human soul and her struggle for salvation was something I knew I needed. Peace of soul—yes, that was what I was seeking, but I found myself afraid. He was so ... Catholic. So conservative. So *right*. Would his wisdom contradict my experiences too? Would the demon come alive in his words? Or worse, be proved to be an angel of God? Would my newfound fragile peace be shattered?

As my homeschooling children swarmed about the house, I stood frozen in the living room. The light played across the floor and on the wood of my desk, inviting me to study, but panic rose and my ribs turned to iron, my breath to fire, my blood to ice as my thumb brushed the edge of the pages. Then with a rush, throwing all at the feet of my generous Jesus, I began to read Fulton's words.

Clarity cut through my mired mind. I grabbed a pen and paper and began writing down quote after quote, as Fulton carefully articulated the truth, slicing between the teaching of the Church and my shadowy demon. Tears slid down my cheeks, a new light dawning in my soul. My heart had not been wrong. Our peaceful fruits had not been wrong.

The gentle warmth of the sunbeam across my desk mirrored the warming in my soul. This beautiful life we had been living *was* from God. I could keep it *and* have Him.

+ + +

Archbishop Fulton Sheen is best known for his brilliant apologetics. Delivered in dramatic style to over thirty million viewers[2] on his TV show *Life is Worth Living*, Sheen took the teachings of the Church and laid them out with both simplicity and depth. Sheen's faith-filled education took him post-ordination to the University of Louvain in Belgium to complete his doctorate in philosophy. Sheen was determined to learn two things: "First, what the modern world is thinking about; second, how to

---

2 Raymond Arroyo, Foreword, *Treasure in Clay: The Autobiography of Fulton J. Sheen,* (New York: Doubleday, 2008), xii.

answer the errors of modern philosophy in the light of the philosophy of St. Thomas."[3] He spent the rest of his life fulfilling these goals.

Sheen was outspoken on the false promises and premises of communism, socialism, and totalitarianism. In seminary during World War I, Sheen's priesthood followed the rise and fall of many dictators and the evils of authoritarian states. He saw their appeal to people's religious principles of brotherhood, sacrifice, and resigning oneself to God's will; he predicted and saw populace after populace duped. "Brotherhood became a revolutionary proletariat; sacrifice became violence, and the Will of God became the will of the dictator."[4]

My shadowy demon was of the same breed. Preying on the goodwill of Catholics committed to Christ, this demon is at work convincing us to submit to a dictatorship. Whether our submission is to our spiritual director, religious group, pastor, or God Himself, as long as we experience our faith through the authoritarian lens, he has succeeded.

How can we know if our spiritual life is governed by authoritarian principles rather than Christ's authority? In *Peace of Soul*, Fulton lays out three clear ways to distinguish the authority of Christ from the authority of Stalin.

First: Authoritarian principles are focused on the external and are often "pressed on one as insistently as a dog barking at the heels of the sheep."[5] *Christ's authority is primarily internal. It respects our reason and our lived experience.*

> "Submission to arbitrary rules that do not coincide with our own best judgment leads to the complete destruction of personality. But the authority of the Church is never arbitrary, never communicated entirely from without; it coincides with the Truth of Christ, which

---

3   Fulton Sheen, *Treasure in Clay: The Autobiography of Fulton J. Sheen* (New York: Doubleday, 2008), 25.

4   Ibid., 93.

5   Fulton Sheen, *Peace of Soul: Timeless Wisdom on Finding Serenity and Joy by the Century's Most Acclaimed Catholic Bishop* (Liguori, MO: Ligouri Publications, 1996). 271.

is already in the soul and which has been accepted on evidence our reason approves. Here the authority accords with our conscience, and it completes the personality that submits to it."[6]

In other words, in true Catholicism, we become more and more deeply ourselves, more infinitely unrepeatable. His Word will not contradict our personality, the demands of our vocation given to us by Him, nor the preferences He has written in our hearts.

Second: A totalitarian leader must suppress the freedom of his followers to ensure that they do not begin to wonder why these principles are discordant with their hearts. Sometimes this is not overt, but a subtle commandeering of our time, energy, or money that leaves us with nothing left over. Christ teaches principles in order that His followers may make wise choices in true freedom. The Ten Commandments leave us an infinitely deep array of choices for painting the canvas of our lives! A totalitarian Christian makes requirements for holiness and claims they are God's. For example, a certain family size, a certain school, daily Mass or Rosary, or participation in certain religious meetings can unfortunately be used to shame fellow Christians into conformity.

Christ never demands conformity; *Christ asks for us to celebrate and live out the unique talents, preferences, and desires that He has placed in our hearts.* He calls each of us to a personal holiness that is designed exactly according to our souls. God tells us to keep Ten Commandments, because that is what can be said to be good for every soul at every time.

Third: The effect of a dictatorship of your soul is fear, anger, or if you reject those because you feel they are not allowed, confusion. When you cross a dictatorship, you become an outcast. Fear of isolation and rejection run deep and can control with the same iron fist as physical imprisonment and torture. *Christ's authority draws out our love.* We are always free to walk away, and the door is always open to returning.

---

6   Ibid.

+ + +

For the first time in over a decade, I was freed to trust myself, to believe that what I experienced so viscerally was real. God was there with me, speaking to me gently—*me*, as me, what I personally needed. Speaking truth into my pain, my joys, my desires and leading me by those very pains, joys, and desires to Himself. He was calling me to embody the Holy Family of Nazareth, in union with Him through entering into family life and marriage and all the littleness of daily life. Through living His Ten Commandments, not a thousand arbitrary rules, my family and I lived in His grace.

In his autobiography, *Treasure in Clay*, Fulton Sheen writes, "I know that I am not afraid to appear before Him. And this is not because I am worthy, nor because I have loved Him with deep intensity, but because *He has loved me*. That is the only reason that any one of us is lovable."[7]

Christ saves us, not because we have saved ourselves, but because He loves us. We do not become Christians because we have slogged over the terrain of the world fashioning our virtue, but rather because we "throb with the very life of God," because the marble of our hearts has burst into bloom.[8] Sheen draws us always back to the heart of Christ: "It is not Christianity ... until one enters the third stage, the Mystical. Here at last—where Christ actually dwells in our hearts, and where there is an awareness rooted in love, and where the soul feels the tremendous impact of God working on itself—here is found the joy that surpasses all understanding."[9]

If we place ourselves under a totalitarian Catholicism, we are seeking peace of mind. We are bringing "some ordering principle to bear on discordant human experiences."[10] "It is precisely because many individuals

---

7   *Treasure in Clay*, 42.
8   *Peace of Soul*, 250.
9   Ibid., 258.
10 Ibid., 275.

are painfully conscious of their weakness and frustration that they yearn for a compulsive system of life that will dispense from them all responsibility, without fully evaluating the reason for their flight."[11] It is comforting to hear that if we check all the boxes, we get to go to heaven. We like to be in control of our final eternal destination; we want certainty about what that big bad God is thinking up there. We don't want the freedom to paint a picture from our soul; we want the Church to host a painting party, where we all paint the same picture according to instruction.

"You are separated from Christ, you who are trying to be justified by law; you have fallen from grace. For through the Spirit, by faith, we await the hope of righteousness."[12]

When we live as true Christians under the authority of Christ, we find ourselves with peace of soul. It is a "True peace … born of the tranquility of order, wherein the senses are subject to the reason, the reason to the faith, and the whole personality to the Will of God."[13] When we are ordered in our whole personality to the Will of God, we are completed by Him. We mirror our infinitesimal piece of God; we are uniquely unrepeatable. We have choices to make, and responsibility to take up, while a loving Father waits breathlessly to see what we will create.

Helen Syski is amazed by the adventures to be had in the wilds of God. A life-long New Englander and Harvard grad, Helen enjoys all four seasons and apple pie with her husband, children, and dogs. She is co-founder of the *Kiss of Mercy Apostolate*, a Little Way to heal the world from abortion. Continue the conversation and download the "Whose Authority Examen" at *AdequateAnthropologist.com*.

---

11   Ibid., 247.
12   Galatians 5: 4–5.
13   *Peace of Soul*, 275.

VI

SHE BELONGS TO YOU

How St. Rose Philippine Duchesne Helped Me to Trust
God with the Outcome of My Apostolic Work

Kristine Bruce

"A friend of yours found me, and I knew in my heart that she belongs to you" was the text I received from my friend Meg one Friday in June, 2022, when her teenage daughter was in Nashville at an estate sale. I was totally puzzled.

Meg's daughter has found a friend of mine? She belongs to me? I thought. *This text makes no sense. What does she possibly mean?*

A minute later a picture arrived from Meg.

I knew at first glance she had found a first class relic of my beloved confirmation saint, St. Rose Philippine Duchesne! My heart skipped a beat. Tears welled in my eyes.

While at the sale, she had seen a table of Catholic items. She took a picture, texted it to her mom, and asked if there was anything she wanted.

Meg spotted the relic in the photo. She couldn't read the name, but she told her daughter to buy it. For eight dollars it was hers.[1]

---

1   The Church forbids the buying and selling of relics. That said, a relic may be "rescued" in cases such as the one in this article. See https://www.catholicnh.org/assets/Documents/Worship/Our-Faith/Understanding/Relics.pdf.

While Meg waited with anticipation to see the relic, she prayed, "Come, Holy Spirit, I realize this relic belongs to someone. Give me the grace to know who."

When her daughter returned home with the relic, Meg recognized the name. In the past I had introduced Meg to St. Philippine (the name she went by), so Meg immediately knew the relic belonged with me! Thank you, Holy Spirit!

Back when I was a teenager, I chose Philippine as my confirmation saint, even though I only knew basic information about her. I knew she was born in France in the 1700s. She came to America to share the Gospel. She founded the school I attended in St. Charles, Missouri.

Now is the time, I thought, *I'm going to find that book I have and learn more about her.*

After ransaking my home, I found the book from 1965 titled, *Philippine Duchesne, Frontier Missionary of the Sacred Heart* by Louise Callan, RSCJ. I dusted it off and began to read.

Rose Philippine Duchesne was born in Grenoble, France, in 1769. She was named after two saints: St. Rose of Lima, the first saint of the Americas, and St. Philip the Apostle. No one could have guessed how her life would emulate these two saints.

One aspect of Philippine's life that surprised me was her father. Pierre-François Duchesne was raised Catholic, but he left the Church after studying politics and law in college. He refused to believe in anything he couldn't fully explain or understand.

Despite her father's lack of faith, Philippine heard the call to religious life and missionary travels by the time of her First Communion when she was twelve. After several years of obstacles and setbacks, God's plan for her came to fruition.

When Philippine was almost nineteen, she entered the Visitation Convent without her parents' permission. However, only a year later, the French government banned all religious vows, and three years later the Visitation Convent was closed. Philippine had to wait eleven years before she could return.

Unfortunately, eleven years of closure had taken a toll on the buildings and the religious. Through a priest, Philippine was encouraged to instead join the Society of the Sacred Heart, which had recently been founded by St. Madeline Sophie Barat in Paris. On November 21, 1805, Philippine made her final vows at the age of thirty-six, twenty-four years after she had heard the calling.

Although Philippine was content in the Society, her desire to be a missionary in the New World continued to grow. She wanted to spread the love of the Sacred Heart to everyone, especially the Native Americans.

Philippine's dreams were inspired by the life of Venerable Mother Mary of the Incarnation, a French Ursuline nun who traveled to Canada in 1639, where she founded the first girls' school in North America and spread the faith among Indigenous and settler communities. Philippine often read about her life and spent hours before the tabernacle praying a prayer written by Mother Mary.

With unwavering faith, Philippine pondered what Jesus said: "Go therefore, and make disciples of all nations" (Matthew 28:19). Nothing was more important to her than sharing Jesus with others.

How truly blessed we shall be if at the price of even very great sacrifices we shall have made God known and loved by one more soul! [2]

For thirteen additional years, Philippine dedicated herself to doing God's will in France. In the Spring of 1817, Bishop Dubourg of New Orleans visited Mother Barat requesting six religious for his diocese in the New World. Philippine desperately knelt before her Mother Superior begging to be sent. Finally, at the age of forty-nine, Philippine made the terrifying seventy-day ocean voyage, determined to "make disciples of all nations." As God would have it, Philippine and her companions landed in New Orleans on May 29, the Feast of the Sacred Heart.

---

2   "Quotes by St. Philippine Duchesne," *Sacred Heart Education*, accessed November 2, 2024, https://www.sacredheartusc.education/mission/founding-mothers/st-philippine-duchesne/quotes-by-st-philippine-duchesne.

Leaving Mother Barat was difficult; however, the sisters communicated regularly via written letters. In one letter, Mother Barat explained what it takes to bring souls to Jesus. She encouraged Philippine to focus on virtues and wrote: "Endeavor to acquire the virtues so necessary for drawing hearts to Christ: meekness, humility, affability, evenness of manner, which is the fruit of patience, and above all that love of Jesus which I so desire to see in you."[3]

At the age of seventy-one, twenty-three years after coming to the New World, Philippine was finally granted the opportunity to serve the Potawatomi people at Sugar Creek, Kansas. By that time, she was quite frail and unable to do the manual work required on the mission. Rather than work, she spent her days and nights in prayer. She prayed so much that the Indians nicknamed her *Quah-kah-ka-num-ad* which means "Woman-who-prays-always."

After only one year at Sugar Creek, she returned to St. Charles for the remaining ten years of her life. Although she definitely kept busy with the students and the Society, she is most remembered for her hours spent in prayer.

When I finished reading her biography, I pondered the question, *What can today's Catholics learn from St. Philippine?*

Philippine died nearly two hundred years ago, yet her example of patience, perseverance, and obedience remain profoundly relevant today. God put on her heart to become a religious missionary when she was only twelve. She waited twenty-four years to make her final vows. She waited thirteen years to travel to the New World. She waited twenty-three years to work with the Potawatomi people. She waited forty-five years for her father's deathbed conversion.

Mother Barat wrote to her, "Well, let us learn to wait, remembering that God's designs are accomplished slowly."[4]

---

3   Louise Callan, RSCJ, *Philippine Duchesne, Frontier Missionary of the Sacred Heart* (New York: Macmillan Company, 1965), 102.

4   Ibid., 103.

Today's Catholics also have to wait. Even though we pray and work, we are called to wait for God's designs to be accomplished, both in our personal stories and in our collective experience. We wait to see an end to abortion, an increased belief in the Real Presence, and a rise in Catholic marriages and baptisms. Alongside these hopes, countless Catholics are waiting for something even closer to home: the return of fallen-away loved ones.

In 2018, I felt the Holy Spirit nudging me to do something to aid in bringing fallen away Catholics back home. *But what?* I prayed.

With the guidance of my spiritual director, a priest, and my best friend, I started a simple apostolate, Praying for Our Prodigals. Similar to Philipppine and Sophie, I send prayers, thoughts, and words of encouragement to help Catholics who are carrying this specific cross.

As I direct this apostolate, I sometimes find myself thinking, *Is anyone reading these emails? Why aren't we seeing more conversions? Why must we wait so long?*

In those moments, my gaze turns to the first class relic of Philippine—a quiet, powerful reminder of God's mysterious ways and a model of patient endurance and surrender of all timing and outcomes to God.

Philippine was a Religious Sister of the Sacred Heart. I attended the first school she founded, the Academy of the Sacred Heart, where I was taught I am "a child of the Sacred Heart."

Somehow, by Divine Providence, this relic found its way to me, not on any ordinary Friday, but on the Solemnity of the Sacred Heart.

I remember Meg's words when she handed me the relic: "I believe it is a consolation and a confirmation for you and your ministry through the Holy Spirit, the Sacred Heart, the Immaculate Heart, and St. Philippine!"

With Meg's words echoing in my heart and Philippine's relic close by, I feel renewed, reminded that this mission is not mine alone but shared with St. Philippine and strengthened by grace. And so, I get back to writing my next email—trusting that even if I don't see every outcome, or if it takes years of unseen efforts and patient endurance, God is working quietly in each soul.

When our desires to serve God do not meet with open doors; when it feels "too late" or futile, when the fruits of our efforts are unseen, St. Philppine's example can encourage us.

Prayer to the Sacred Heart of Jesus

by Venerable Mother Mary of the Incarnation
(1599–1672)

By the Heart of my Jesus, who is the Way, the Truth, and the Life, I approach Thee, O Eternal Father.

By this Divine Heart, I adore Thee, for those who do not adore Thee; I love Thee for all who do not love Thee; I acknowledge Thee as my God, for all the willfully blind, who through contempt refuse to acknowledge Thee.

By this Divine Heart, I desire to pay Thee the homage which all Thy creatures owe Thee. In spirit I go round the wide world, in search of the souls redeemed by the precious blood of Jesus. I present them all to Thee through Him, and by His merits I ask for their conversion.

O Eternal Father! wilt Thou permit them to remain in ignorance of my Jesus? Wilt Thou suffer that they should not live for him who died for all? Thou sees, O Heavenly Father! that they live not yet; grant them then life, by this Divine Heart.

Through this adorable Heart I present Thee all who labor for the extension of the Gospel, that by its merits, they may be replenished with Thy Holy Spirit.

On it, as on a Divine Altar, I present to Thee especially (insert names of loved ones here).

Thou knowest, O Incarnate Word, my adorable Saviour! that all that I would ask Thy Father by Thy Divine Heart, by Thy Holy soul. I ask it of Thee, when I ask it of Him, because Thou art in Thy Father, and Thy Father is in Thee.

Deign together to hear my prayer, and to make the souls whom I present to Thee, one with Thee. Amen.[5]

---

5 *The Life of Mother Mary of the Incarnation; A Religious of the Ursuline Community* (1677), 148.

Kristine Bruce has been called to support, encourage, and pray with Catholics whose loved ones have left the Church. Every Friday, she shares messages of guidance, prayer, and hope to uplift and strengthen Catholics amid the trials of wayward loved ones. For a touch of comfort and connection (and even her all-time favorite cookie recipe!), visit *PrayingForOurProdigals.com*.

VII

A Mother's Saint

How St. Gerard Majella Joined My Intercessory Army

Shauna Occhipinti

Amid the steady beeps of his NICU monitors, my son outstretched his tiny translucent hand. His palm settled on my chest, just below my sterling silver St. Gerard medal, and remained there for the next two hours.

He had been overheating in his isolette. "Can you hold him tonight, skin to skin, to help regulate his temperature?" the NICU nurse asked. "Of course," I exclaimed, settling into the chair, grateful for any opportunity to cradle my new son.

I was helping regulate his fragile body, but his palm, not much bigger than my St. Gerard medal, was regulating my mom-heart. His hand rose and fell with each of my breaths. There wasn't much I could do for him or his twin brother in the NICU except to be present—silently begging heaven for help, especially St. Gerard. My petitions mingled with prayers of thanksgiving among those hallowed hospital walls.

I met St. Gerard years earlier, during my anguished infertility journey. My mom gave me a prayer card introducing him as the patron saint of motherhood (one saint among many in this patronage) and of those who wanted to become mothers. I quietly gathered him into my intercessory army and implored him to plead my case before God.

This devotion wasn't one I shared with others, except for my Catholic Infertility Yahoo group (long before the days of high-speed Internet and Facebook). St. Gerard was an intercessor I held close to my barren heart. I asked for his help during my weekly Adoration hour. I called upon him with my shattered heart when another monthly reminder of *no new life* arrived. I begged him to ask Jesus, the Divine Physician, to heal me. I asked to be one of his "motherhood miracles."

Month after month and year after year passed. The answer to those prayers didn't come—at least not in the way or in the time I expected.

Then, one Saturday morning, the phone rang. "You were chosen," a voice exclaimed.

Suddenly my empty arms and barren womb were full. I was blessed with twin sons through the miracle of adoption. They were born extremely premature at twenty-seven weeks and in a city three hours away from home. Their births ushered in a new season of intense prayers.

A few weeks into their NICU stay, my in-laws traveled to see us and meet their new grandsons. My mother-in-law quietly pulled me aside and placed a St. Gerard necklace into my hands.

I was perplexed. She wasn't Catholic.

I listened intently as she shared the story of this necklace. Long before I was born, St. Gerard was weaving his way into my life through the Italian family I would one day call my own.

When my mother-in-law tragically lost her first son at birth, her Italian Catholic mother-in-law gave this St. Gerard necklace to her. For all these years, she had quietly held onto it.

"I thought you might like it now," she said, not knowing if I would even recognize who this saint was.

My eyes filled with tears. "Thank you." With shaking hands, I clasped the necklace around my neck. "I've asked for his intercession for years."

I wore that St. Gerard necklace during our sons' two-month NICU stay. Their tiny hands grasped it as we rocked through many skin-to-skin "kangaroo care" hours.

During their precarious first year of life, I held the cold silver disc between my thumbs like a prayer lifeline to my special heavenly helper who I knew was interceding for me and my family.

St. Gerard was born on April 6, 1726, in Muro Lucano, Italy, a town about fifty miles south of Naples, Italy. He was born to Benedetta and Dominico Majella. From his unusually easygoing manner as a baby to his preoccupation with spiritual matters in his early years, Gerard's piety drew attention.

For fun, young Gerard organized religious processions with neighborhood children, constructed home altars, imitated the prayers and gestures from Mass, and placed photos of saints around his home. He often ate little in an offer of mortification, which understandably concerned his mother. Her friends consoled her saying that "he was a child of heaven."[1] His entire life bore witness to this.

At just five years old, he knelt in the chapel of Capotignano, near a statue of the Blessed Mother holding the child Jesus. Suddenly, the statue of the child Jesus came to life, left his mother's arms, and began playing with Gerard.

I know, I know... But there's more. The child also gave Gerard a loaf of white bread, which he took home. Gerard returned to the chapel daily, and the scene repeated itself. Perplexed about where this daily bread was coming from, his sister, Brigida, and his mother both followed him and witnessed the miraculous scene.

"Give us this day our daily bread" (Matthew 6:11) was happening quite literally in Gerard's young life.

---

1 Father Edward Saint-Omar, C.SS.R., *Saint Gerard Majella: The Wonder-Worker and Patron of Expectant Mothers*, 13.

Maybe this mystical experience cultivated his hunger for the Eucharist—a hunger that continued growing for the rest of his life. He was often found sitting for hours in front of the Blessed Sacrament. His ecstatic love for Our Lord led to him levitating in the presence of the Eucharist.

When Gerard was around twelve, his father died. To help provide for his family, Gerard left school to work. Despite challenging work conditions and a deep desire to join a religious order, Gerard was a faithful and diligent worker focused on pleasing God in all he did.

While still a teen, Gerard asked to join the Capuchins, but was turned away due to frail health. At twenty-two, he was quickly, but reluctantly, admitted to the Congregation of the Most Holy Redeemer—the Redemptorists—as a lay brother. This "useless" new brother quickly surprised everyone with his deep wisdom, ardent love, work ethic, happiness in suffering, and extraordinary gifts. But God wasn't surprised.

Our Lord had showered supernatural gifts upon Gerard almost from birth. Gerard placed those gifts at the service of Christ and His Church.

He had the gifts of bilocation, prophecy, discernment of spirits, vision at a distance, ecstasies, infused knowledge, power over nature, healing, conversion, and reading sinners' hearts, among others. Astounding, isn't it, that all these gifts were active in one young man!

Gerard didn't keep these gifts to himself. He allowed them to overflow and bless others.

Unlike the hidden saints, Gerard became a well-known and sought-after presence in his community and beyond. Word of him as a "wonder-worker" spread quickly. He couldn't enter a town without people running toward him exclaiming, "The saint is here." And yet he remained humble and always redirected others to Jesus.

One of the many miracles that earned him the title of *"the Mother's Saint"* took place shortly before his death. Gerard was visiting friends. As he left their home, one of the daughters ran after him. He had forgotten his handkerchief.

"Keep it," he told the girl. "It will be useful to you some day."[2]

Many years later, this same girl found her life in danger during childbirth. She recalled St. Gerard's words and requested the handkerchief. When it was placed on her, the pain miraculously ceased, her life was spared, and she gave birth to a healthy baby. This miracle was only one of many that expectant mothers experienced from St. Gerard's intercession.

On October 16, 1755, Gerard died from tuberculosis at the young age of twenty-nine. In his last days, his intense and isolating physical suffering brought him intimately close to the wounds of our Lord. Just as he lived, uniting his entire self—body, mind, and soul—with Our Lord, so too he died.

As he lay on his death bed, hemorrhaging and in excruciating pain, he had a sign placed on his door. "Here we do the will of God, as God wills it and as long as God wills it."[3]

Gerard was beatified by Pope Leo XIII on January 29, 1893, and canonized by St. Pius X on December 11, 1904.

His feast day is celebrated on October 16. He shares this feast day with St. Margaret Mary Alacoque. She lived almost a hundred years earlier and is known for spreading devotion to the Sacred Heart of Jesus, a devotion that was also dear to St. Gerard. "Let us remain always in the Sacred Heart of Jesus," he wrote to a Mother Superior. "In this Heart is found all sweetness, and there is rest."[4]

Gerard spent his life in total obedience to the will of God. He didn't question God's will, even when it brought great suffering. He wanted everyone to understand that true happiness is only found when we unite our will with God's will—a lesson we desperately need in our world today.

I needed that lesson in my own life too when I first met St. Gerard. I had one idea about how and when God should bless me with the gift of

---

2   Father Edward Saint-Omar, C.SS.R., *Saint Gerard Majella: The Wonder-Worker and Patron of Expectant Mothers*, 211.

3   Ibid., 179.

4   Ibid., 63.

motherhood. When I finally surrendered my will to His, when I learned to trust God's timing and God's ways, when I conformed my will to His, He brought blessings beyond worldly satisfaction.

He wants you to experience this true happiness too.

When I read that St. Gerard was from southern Italy, not far from where my mother-in-law's mother-in-law was from, I smiled. I am no longer surprised at the beautiful tapestry St. Gerard has woven among my family over generations.

Last August, when my boys headed off to college hundreds of miles from home, I retrieved my precious St. Gerard necklace and clasped it around my neck once again. When my mom-anxiety choked me, and I would feel the boys' absence most acutely, my fingers flew to this silver reminder of my special saint.

God is faithful. His timing and His plans are always perfect. No matter what you are facing today, no matter how you are suffering, He is here. He simply asks for your obedience, for your trust, and for your heart.

St. Gerard, thank you for showing us how to live in close union with God. May we always, "Love God greatly; be always united to God; do everything for God; love everything for God," as you taught.[5]

Thank you for the wonders you are still working today as you accompany us in this vale of tears.

I ask for your intercession for all the women silently suffering with infertility—that God would grant them the desire of their hearts. I pray for all the birth moms whose sacrifices make the gift of motherhood possible for women like me. I pray for my mom, my mother-in-law and my grandmother-in-law and the tapestry of faith and family that St. Gerard wove through us. And I pray for all the moms of young adults who are being invited to new heights in their surrendered trust.

---

5 *Meditative Novena to Saint Gerard Majella: His Writings and Spirituality*, Redemptorist Pastoral Publication.

Maybe you are not a mom. Maybe you have never dealt with infertility. St. Gerard still wants to be your friend and heavenly intercessor. In addition to motherhood and pregnancy, he is also the patron saint of the falsely accused, good confessions, the pro-life movement, and lay brothers. St. Gerard continues working wonders and drawing others close to the heart of Jesus. Ask him to intercede for you. Boldly call upon him, and then wait in complete confidence, ready to follow wherever God leads.

Traditional St. Gerard Prayer for Motherhood

O good St Gerard, powerful intercessor before God and wonder worker of our day, confidently I call upon you and seek your aid. On earth you always fulfilled God's designs, help me now to do the holy will of God. Implore the Master of Life, from whom all parenthood proceeds, to render me fruitful in offspring, that I may raise up children to God in this life, and in the world to come, heirs to the Kingdom of His Glory. Amen.

Shauna Occhipinti writes to bear witness to the One who has transformed her life. She loves helping women find time for contemplation and prayer through leading SoulCore Rosary classes, organizing retreats, and facilitating a Well-Read Mom's group. Find out more at *shaunaocchipinti.com*.

VIII

Unwavering Faith

How St. Martha Taught Me the Better Part

Barb Lishko

Inhaling deeply, the mountain air filled my nostrils, and I smiled. We had returned the day before to our *little piece of heaven* deep in the pines of Colorado. That morning, we were hosting Fr. Sam and Fr. Dan for breakfast. When the doorbell rang, I gave the bacon a quick flip and answered the door, expecting a technician to hook up our Internet.

The workers were right on time and went to work. I hastily continued preparations. Time was of the essence, as our guests would arrive soon.

Another knock. Another question regarding placement and wiring. I was starting to feel nervous that I wouldn't finish the meal preparations in time, but I led the workman through the house to the back door. Immediately blinded by the rising sun's light, I failed to stop and let my eyes adjust. Missing the step, I landed hard in an ugly fall, sprawled out on the deck. Searing pain blasted through my right foot.

The workman stared at me, not knowing what to do. Finally, he helped me into a chair. I tried to catch my breath and not panic. He returned to his work while I tried not to pass out. The delicious aroma of bacon wafted through the window and acted like smelling salts as I snapped awake and remembered the stove was still on. I hopped to the door.

It was locked.

Fear flowed through me as I imagined the bacon grease igniting the open gas flames. *Thanks, Lord*, I thought sarcastically. *I was just trying to feed your hungry priests.*

I hollered to the teen assisting the crew who was passing by. "Hey there, I need your help. I'm locked out of the house and need to get back in." Giving him the code to our garage, he found his way to the back door.

Once inside, I hopped over to the stove, shut off the bacon, and crawled to the nearest chair to text my husband, who by now was almost home with the priests. I simply wrote, "Advil, ice, and an Ace bandage. Martha is down for the count. You're making breakfast."

"But Martha was distracted with much serving; and she went to [Jesus] and said, 'Lord, do you not care that my sister has left me to serve alone? Tell her then to help me'" (Luke 10:40).

I am in good company when it comes to hospitality. Like St. Martha, and many of us, I *need to feed* people. It started off harmlessly enough with meals for our growing family. Once our children entered Catholic school, the ground was ripe for this passion to grow. Soon, my endeavor encompassed parish festivals, school fundraisers, and special events. I became Martha resurrected.

When we moved back to Arizona to be near family, the only thing that didn't change was my willingness to volunteer at our parish. Experience coupled with the ability to feed hundreds and my inability to say "no," created the perfect recipe for a dedicated volunteer.

Continually pouring yourself out for others has the potential to breed resentment. If God is not the key ingredient in every gift of yourself, it will fail to yield bountiful fruit. I know this firsthand.

I looked to Martha as my mentor and guide in learning to rely more on Christ and less on myself. When overwhelmed, she knew exactly who to turn to; Jesus was always the answer for her and should also be for us.

Jesus recognized Martha's efforts to feed his hungry band of disciples by offering genuine hospitality. We can easily fall into the trap of thinking no one notices or cares about our well-intentioned efforts.

The Liar and Enemy of our souls capitalizes on this insecurity by feeding off our already wounded feelings and pulling up past infractions by others.

It is critical that we recognize this interior whisper when it begins and take it to the Lord. As Fr. Jacque Philippe writes, "Our freedom always has the marvelous power to make what is taken from us—by life, events, or other people—into something offered. Externally there is no visible difference, but internally everything is transfigured."[1]

Rarely are we able to control everything that happens in life, but we can control how we respond by making unplanned situations an offering to God rather than an occasion for self-pity.

The truth is that nothing we do for others goes unnoticed by Christ.

We first hear about Martha in the Gospel of St. Luke. Martha was the first to welcome Jesus and his disciples to her home. She had a sister named Mary and a brother, Lazarus. They lived in Bethany.

Fr. Roger Landry, in his homily to the Visitation Convent of the Sisters of Life on the feast day of St. Martha in 2017 reminds us, "Together with St. Benedict, she is the most famous saint of hospitality in the history of the Church." What an incredible honor for her and those of us who make her come to life in our hospitality efforts.

Christ knew her by name and was a frequent guest at Martha's home in Bethany. Scripture records three visits in Luke 10:38–42, John 11:1–53, and John 12:1–9. St. Martha also left us a compelling witness of faith by how she responded to Jesus after her brother Lazarus died. She demonstrates a faith that does not wait for proof. She models what confidence in God looks and sounds like.

Tradition tells us that, after the first persecutions of Christians, St. Martha, with Mary, Lazarus, and other disciples, left their own land and went to France, arriving in Saintes-Maries-de-la-Mer, in Provence, where they brought the Christian faith. The liturgical memorial of St. Martha

---

1   Fr. Jacques Philippe, *Interior Freedom*. Translated by Helen Scott (New York: Scepter, 2007).

was begun by Franciscans in 1262, who celebrated her feast on July 29, eight days after the feast of her sister, St. Mary Magdalene.

"But the Lord answered her, 'Martha, Martha, you are anxious and troubled about many things; one thing is needful. Mary has chosen the good portion, which shall not be taken away from her'" (Luke 10:41–42).

Ouch! Where did Martha go wrong?

Christ wanted to teach Martha—and by extension, all of us—that despite all the good work we do, we need to recognize a precious opportunity for something better, something eternal.

> As Pope Francis asks, "Why then was Martha scolded, even if kindly, by Jesus? Because she considered only what she was doing to be essential, she was too absorbed and worried by the things 'to do.' For a Christian, works of service and charity are never detached from the principle of all our action: that is, listening to the Word of the Lord."

Some fruits are not measured by productivity alone. Take the case of Mary sitting at the feet of Christ for example.[2]

Martha had the privilege of serving Jesus but was completely unaware that this moment held a precious and more incredible privilege, to sit and be fed herself. We too can often be so absorbed in the details of hospitality for "others" that we miss the gift intended for us by drawing closer to Christ; which requires we are still and receptive.

Like Martha, we can fail to see that Jesus's primary interest is in pursuing *our* hearts.

It may have seemed ungrateful and cruel for the Lord to call her out giving kudos only to Mary, but it was done in love for her greater good. *"But [Jesus] answered, 'It is written, "Man shall not live by bread alone, but by every word that proceeds from the mouth of God"'"* (Matthew 4:4).

Physical food is good, but soul food is better. Jesus sought to remind Martha, and by extension, me, that all my work and effort, while valuable,

---

2   Pope Francis, Angelus address, July 21, 2013.

if not connected to Him, was futile. Like Martha, I needed to be fed first before attempting to feed others, to work from a full heart rather than an empty one. Things changed in my faith, life, and ministry when I began to be intentional about these efforts.

"Martha said to Jesus, 'Lord, if you had been here, my brother would not have died. And even now I know that whatever you ask from God, God will give you'" (John 11;21–22).

Martha's faith in Christ was unwavering. She demonstrated that she had learned the lesson Christ desired to teach her.

Thankfully, Martha taught me that the better part involves receiving and being fed first. What does that look like? Feeding on the Word of God in Scripture, reading about the saints and most important the Bread of Life, is where I have learned what love demands of me as His beloved daughter. It is befitting that what I consume, consumes and transforms me. Rather than merely seeing tasks to accomplish, I see hearts in need of Christ's authentic love. St. Martha's example has been instrumental in how I share my talents in the kitchen and invite others into deeper relationships with Christ through my writing.

Who would believe God would use feeding and serving as the impetus that firmly secured my future in Church ministry and the transformation of my own heart? How I gathered people led to more profound encounters in faith. Food and hospitality were the keys that unlocked hearts toward encountering Christ.

+ + +

Recently, because of these very gifts, I was asked to mentor the young woman who would manage the new coffee shop at our parish. Our pastor hoped to make it a place of welcome and fellowship for our community.

Months of planning and renovation had produced a beautiful environment, and we were ready to get down to the workings of the *back of the house*, where she had no prior experience. A small private gathering would be an excellent opportunity to put into practice what we had been preparing for. The following week was the grand opening.

Together, we readied the necessary food and beverages, and the meeting began. After some time, I started doing what any good hostess does: bussing tables and refilling platters. But where was my sweet Mary? She was sitting among the guests and visiting. Making eye contact and smiling, without resentment, I gently whispered to her, "Get up. Your role here today is to be Martha, not Mary."

What came intuitively for me over years of experience was a new paradigm for her. Without Martha's example and guidance over all these years, I may have gotten frustrated or harsh. The Eucharist daily at Mass has been the game changer, and through Adoration, I too can sit at his feet. I can be the best of Martha yet have a heart like Mary. Thank you, St. Martha.

Prayer to St. Martha

Dearest St. Martha, friend of Jesus, you have taught me by your example to welcome and receive Jesus in the home of my heart. I cannot give what I do not possess, so must rely completely on Jesus, the source and fountain of every good effort. Placing myself at the service of Jesus helps me to welcome and receive the stranger in His Name.

St. Martha increase my capacity to love as you did. And, in imitation of you, may I confess with boldness and surety that Jesus is Lord and Savior through all my work.

St. Martha, pray for us. Amen.

Barb Lishko loves to bring others closer to Jesus through good food, fellowship, and the written word. Her reflections are filled with stories both humorous and sublime from the antics of family life through ministry to the engaged and married. She is a speaker, writer, and natural-born Martha. Barb is married and blessed with grandbabies. She invites you to read her reflections via her blog: *BarbLishko.com.*

IX

NOTHING WOULD EVER BE THE SAME

How Mary Undoer of Knots Worked
a Miracle in My Motherhood

Kate Eschbach

Sundays were my favorite: church choir, volunteering in the nursery, lunch with my best friend as we drove to Lake Lewisville for the afternoon, followed by choir practice and youth group. Sundays were predictable and perfect. I had a place to belong, and it was lovely.

I hoped my children would have the same experience—solid and holy friendships filled with silly skits, laughter, and hearts that knew unconditional love even in their awkward teenage years. Moreso, I wanted to be a part of all of it—I loved being a mom and had dreamed of having a large family, but God had other plans. After two children, I experienced miscarriages and struggled with infertility, which was a bitter cross but one I had surrendered to carrying. I found healing for my heart during the adoption process for our little redhead, Riley. Although I still yearned for a large family, I resolved not to miss a moment of the motherhood I *had* been granted.

In 2014, I was thrilled to have the opportunity to be a chaperone for my eldest daughter's summer youth group retreat. I tried not to let her know how absolutely giddy I was at the opportunity to practice what I had been preparing for my entire life: youth group counselor extraordinaire. I thought of Tim Morrison and John Baldwin, the choir director and youth director, respectively, who had taken my childhood youth group on countless excursions in an old white van. Mission trips to New Mexico and choir trips to Colorado and Myrtle Beach filled my summer with equal parts of acts of service and the gift of friendship. Our youth group eventually graduated to a proper bus, but our love for ridiculously loud camp songs transferred effortlessly to our updated ride.

I snapped a selfie and proudly wrote a caption about being the chaperone, and I settled in for our journey to Tucson, Arizona, for Steubenville West.

I tried my very best to steer clear of my daughter at meal times and small devotional times, to give her space to befriend and discover the wonderful world of retreats without me. We sang loudly, listened to inspiring talks, and made a burger run at eleven p.m.

My excitement began to cool when I realized that I would be sleeping in a University of Arizona dorm room in a raised twin bed. I was slightly terrified that if I rolled over too quickly in the middle of the night, I might find myself facedown on the very worn carpet floor.

Although we had fun, I missed the comforts of home and decided I had probably waited too long to begin my foray into youth counseling.

On Saturday evening, Mass was followed by two hours of Eucharistic Adoration, which was what I had been waiting for! Praise and worship music filled the air as over 2,000 high school students knelt in front of Jesus. Adoration began, and Father Louis Merosne began processing with the monstrance throughout the auditorium. Our group was on the second-floor balcony. I had never experienced Adoration as I did that evening.

I alternated between singing loudly and sitting in silence as I listened to young voices praise God in song. I thanked God for blessings—so many blessings. After a year of uncertainty around Riley's adoption, we had just been given the official court date. I had so much to be grateful for. What more could I want? Only one other thing. A deep desire had begun to stir within me, not for any blessings, but for Jesus Himself.

As I watched Father Louis Merosne, I wondered if he would carry the Monstrance up to the balcony. I wanted to see Jesus up close. I wanted to breathe deeply as He walked by and thank Him with every fiber of my heart. I began to feel a deep desire to find *Him*.

The balcony seemed very dark as I looked around, but suddenly the spotlight shined on the stairs to stage left, where we were, and then He was there! This was my chance! I wondered if this is what the woman at the well felt when Jesus drew near. I wanted to touch His garment and thank Him.

As Father passed by, I began laughing uncontrollably. I covered my mouth with my hands. There was nothing I could do to stop the joy that was bubbling out of me. My daughter smiled and hugged me tightly. Our youth minister's wife, Karen, smiled. She leaned over and took my shoulders. "Don't worry! This happens sometimes! It is just because He loves you so much."

I gave in and laughed and sang as tears streamed down my cheeks.

I didn't want my joy to end.

That moment was punctuated equilibrium, a time in my life when nothing would or could ever be the same again.

As Adoration finished, Father Louis walked up to the stage and said that someone present was struggling with infertility. He smiled. "God has just untied the knots." I looked around and assumed it was one of the youth ministers. After all, he couldn't be talking about the teenagers, right?

We traveled home the next day, and I collapsed on the couch. The dirty laundry would have to wait another day. I announced that the retreat had been amazing, and I was thankful for the opportunity, but that I was exhausted, and just too old to be trying to stay up as late as the teenagers.

As I settled back into family life and we prepared for our adoption to be finalized, I took Riley to TJ Maxx, where he proudly danced around the three-way mirror in his khaki pants and navy button-down shirt. He looked so handsome, I couldn't help but grin and share his joy. His face lit up when he realized that he was wearing the same outfit as his older brother. His red curls made me smile.

Two months later, we were in a courtroom when the judge announced, "Congratulations! It's a boy!" We all laughed and hugged our three-year-old son. My parents had traveled from Texas to Arizona for the ceremony, and we all decided to find a yummy breakfast as we continued celebrating becoming a family of five. Riley's grandmother and great aunt went with us. I wanted his grandmother and great aunt to know that they had become a part of our family too. The world seemed beautiful and bright and calm on that September morning.

As we were walking to breakfast, my mom slowly walked next to me. She held my arm, patted my hand, and and asked how I was. I told her that I actually didn't feel well, which I attributed to the stress of the paperwork and court dates and the delays we had faced.

Mom stopped walking and looked me in the eye and said, "Sweetheart, you need to take a pregnancy test."

"What?" I stared at her wide-eyed. "Mom, you know that isn't even possible."

Brian and I had been told years ago, after many miscarriages (twelve years of miscarriages to be exact) that I would never carry to term again.

Mom smiled as we ate breakfast. I silently wondered if this could be happening. With the miscarriages, I didn't have morning sickness, but over the past weeks, I was barely able to eat or drink anything.

I told Brian about Mom's suspicions on the ride home, so he said we would celebrate either way and bought ice cream and champagne.

That evening, after two lines appeared on the test, we *all* laughed hysterically as we ate ice cream around our dining room table, realizing that we wouldn't be a family of five for long. The following April, we added baby number four.

I remembered what Father Louis had said. Knots ... *Was it me? Was I the one whose knots were untied as Jesus passed by? Had twelve years of miscarriage suddenly been healed during Adoration? Was that why my heart was bursting with joy?*

I asked my eldest daughter and our youth director's wife, Karen, if they remembered what Father Louis had said after Adoration. They did.

Karen told me about Mary, Undoer of Knots. I began to learn more and more about Our Blessed Mother under this title.

I discovered that a German artist, Johann Melchior Georg Schmittdner, painted the image now titled "Mary, Undoer of Knots" around 1700 after being inspired by a meditation of St. Irenaeus, who expanded on the parallel St. Paul drew between Adam and Christ. St. Irenaus made a similar comparison when he pointed out that "Eve, by her disobedience, tied the knot of disgrace for the human race, whereas Mary, by her obedience, undid it"[1]. The image had been venerated in Germany for hundreds of years, and Pope Francis came to love the devotion while in Germany in the 1980s and brought it back to Argentina. After he became pope, it spread throughout the world, and the faithful now look to Our Lady under this title to untie the seemingly impossible "knots" in their lives.

That April, we named our daughter Mary Alice in honor of my mother and grandmother, and in honor of Mary, Undoer of Knots.

God had indeed untied the knots that night.

+ + +

Is there a situation that seems so tangled that you aren't sure where to turn? Maybe it is painful, and you have stopped praying about it and decided to give up praying about it. I invite you to ask the Holy Spirit to reveal what wound your heart needs to be healed from.

Join me in asking Our Lady to untie the knots in your life.

---

1   *Against the Heresies*, Book V, Chapter 19

Prayer to Mary, Undoer of Knots

O Holy Mary, Undoer of Knots, you have a mother's heart that untangles the knots in our lives. We come before you today, entrusting you with the tangled ribbon of our lives.

O Mary Undoer of Knots, take into your hands the knots that bind us:

The knots of discord in our families,
The knots of misunderstanding between loved ones,
The knots of unemployment and financial strain,
The knots of illness and suffering,
The knots of addiction and despair,
The knots of past mistakes that haunt us still,
The knots that we have hidden away and forgotten.

Gentle Mother, you who know how to untangle even the most difficult knots, loosen the bonds that constrain us. With your graceful fingers, release us from the snares and complications that distress our souls.

Intercede for us, O Mary Undoer of Knots, that through your powerful mediation, we may find peace, clarity, and resolution. Help us to see the way forward when all seems dark and confused.

Teach us to persevere with faith and hope, trusting in God's infinite wisdom and love. Guide our steps along the path of holiness and truth.

We thank you, Mary Undoer of Knots, for hearing our prayer. We know that you never fail those who place their trust in you. Untie the knots in our lives, that we may give glory to God and serve Him with joy. Amen.

Kate Eschbach is a blogger, speaker, micro-influencer, photographer, and podcast host of *Tripping Over the Saints*. She loves to create community and encourage others. She will tell anyone who stands still about the miracle that happened in her life. She is a Catholic convert, wife to her college sweetheart, and mom of five. You can find her at *SongsKateSang.com*.

X

CHAMPION OF THE FAMILY ROSARY

How Venerable Fr. Patrick Peyton helped
me Embrace My Primary Vocation

Christine Rich

I was finally ready to leave the security of his well-worn leather recliner, so I pulled myself up, walked down the hallway, and out the door. As I crossed the parking lot to my car, I felt as if a great burden was being lifted—as if chains, shackles, or the heavy armored scales of a dragon, were being shed from me, dropping away and crashing to the pavement with a loud clanging.

Have I been held captive without even knowing it?

Earlier that morning, after our monthly Mass in the small chapel on the property of The Little Sisters of the Poor in San Pedro, California, I had announced that I would be leaving the company that I had co-founded. Sharing the stories of saints and the power of prayer at My Saint My Hero Catholic jewelry company had been my life's work.

I left the chapel after my announcement and took refuge in my favorite place of prayer and peace: one of the bedrooms in the retreat center on the property of the Little Sisters of the Poor, where Venerable Fr. Patrick Peyton, the Rosary priest and champion of families, had lived out the last three years of his life. He had been cared for by the Little Sisters until he passed into eternal life in 1992.

I entered Fr. Peyton's room hoping to regain the peace I had always felt in this sacred space. Time stood still in this room; nothing had changed nor been moved since his death. I sank into his leather armchair, a place where I had prayed for hours in the years that I had the privilege of time alone there. Once again, I was drawn to Fr. Peyton's favorite painting of Our Blessed Mother that sat on his desk. I had no doubt that she had led me to Fr. Peyton, knowing that he would lead me to her Son, Jesus.

Fr. Patrick Peyton was born on January 9, 1909, one of nine children on a small farm in County Mayo, Ireland. He grew up in a family surrounded by faith. His dream had been to become a missionary priest, but he had left school after sixth grade and was told he was not smart enough to become one.

So Patrick decided to follow the American dream and asked his brother to go to Philadelphia with him, where he hoped to become a millionaire. After months of searching, the only job Patrick could land in Philly was as a janitor in the local cathedral. In the quiet, alone with God and his broom, his desire to become a priest grew once again.

He and his brother were both invited to become priests with the Congregation of the Holy Cross and study at Notre Dame University, but once again Patrick's plans were put on hold as he became sick and was hospitalized with a case of tuberculosis that doctors said was incurable. After almost a year in the hospital with great pain and suffering, and the doctors telling him his condition was hopeless, his mentor from the seminary paid him a visit to encourage him.

"You have the faith, Pat," he said. "But you're not using it."[1] He reminded him of the great faith of his mother back in Ireland and told him to pray to the Blessed Mother with all his heart.

---

1   Family Rosary, Father Patrick Peyton, CSC: The Rosary Priest, "*Coming to America, Immigrant to Priest*," October 20, 2024, https://www.fatherpeyton.org/chapters/chapter-2

Summoning up all his faith, Patrick did just that, and shortly after, he felt a lifting of the darkness, depression, and pain. He knew he had been cured. The doctors confirmed his miracle, and he was ordained with his brother the next spring. From then on, Fr. Peyton was determined to spend the rest of his life "giving his heart and soul for the love of Mary."[2]

Fr. Peyton passionately described how the sight of both of his parents on their knees praying with their rosary beads at the end of each long day taught him about the power of family prayer. "This is family love, and I thank the family Rosary for it!"[3] he proclaimed. Out of this love for families and the Blessed Mother, he announced that he was going to get ten million families to pledge to say the Rosary together. His Family Rosary Crusade was born.

Like Fr. Peyton's mother, I will never forget the magenta rosary that my mother had in her hand every day when she drove me to school. She told me the story of the Rosary Priest whose slogan she repeated often: "The family that prays together stays together." Yet, even with her beautiful example, I never made it a priority to pray the Rosary.

After I was married and had four children, I went on a pilgrimage and had an encounter with our Blessed Mother that deepened my faith and changed my heart forever. Before this trip, the faith of my family had been based on the fact that we went to Mass every Sunday and our children attended Catholic school. I had a group of friends that I prayed the Rosary with weekly, but as I encountered Jesus in a new way on this trip, I realized that I was not answering my call as a mother and wife; I needed to bring a deeper life of prayer into my home. I had a desire to pray the Rosary with my family, but at the same time I was worried they would think I had become a "crazy church lady," so I didn't have the courage to suggest it to them.

---

2   Ibid.
3   Family Rosary, Father Patrick Peyton C.S.C., "*The Impassioned Apostle*", Oct 20, 2024, https://youtu.be/_5RKhBfuQbg?si=CSY-Xm6Gbb-2Q8w8

Unbeknownst to me, God had a plan. During that pilgrimage, I was given a penance after confession with a faithful priest to pray every night with my family—just one Our Father, three Hail Marys and one Glory Be; the beginning of a rosary! Starting with just these few prayers didn't seem too much to propose to them.

I returned home, and with a little push from Mother Mary, I gathered my husband and four children around the bed of our youngest daughter and we started.

At first, praying together felt awkward and didn't always feel holy. Some nights, my teenage son sat with an angsty look on his face, wondering when it would be over. On other nights, as it was getting late, my husband could be heard yelling down our hallway, "Are we going to pray, or what?!"

Through all of the normality of family life, we started to notice a change. Our two middle daughters in junior high no longer fought daily, and we noticed them sticking up for each other at school. The daily background of yelling and squabbling in our household seemed to be fading away.

Our youngest always remained our anchor in this time of prayer. Her belief in the power of prayer was edifying as she would rattle off all the prayer requests she brought home from school. She was convicted and she inspired us all.

The change became real when we were driving to Sunday Mass one morning after a tumultuous time of getting the family out the door—my husband said quietly to me, "I think we need to start praying together again." He had noticed that we had grown lax in praying as a family and the old family habits had crept back in.

I couldn't help but remember the words from the Rosary priest my mom had told me: "The family that prays together, stays together.[4]" I had watched this transformation become real in my own home.

---

4   Holy Cross Family Ministries, *Father Peyton's Rosary Prayers* (San Francisco: Ignatius Press, 2005), 8.

Close friends and family commented to me, "I wish my kids loved each other the way yours do. What's your secret?"

"Prayer," I answered. "We just pray these simple prayers together every night, that's it. You should try it!"

Then one day when I was visiting the Little Sisters of the Poor for daily Mass, one of the sisters asked if I had ever seen Fr. Peyton's room. "Fr. Peyton, from the Family Rosary Crusade?!" I couldn't believe what I was hearing. By this time, Fr. Peyton had become my hero.

I had started praying with him by listening online to the old recordings of him praying the Rosary with Mother Teresa, Fulton Sheen, Bing Crosby, Lucille Ball, Frank Sinatra, and an endless list of others. He had become my spiritual partner in prayer, and praying along with him helped me pray the Rosary every day.

When the sweet sister heard what a fan I was of Fr. Peyton, she gave me an open invitation to "visit with him" at any time. I took refuge there often and took my children along to teach them about him. We sat on the floor in his room and prayed the Rosary, as if he were right there with us.

"Mere reason did not tell Mary that Jesus was God. When she saw her Son dying on the Cross, Mary didn't get to *see* that Jesus was our Savior ... she *believed* it.[5]" I had meditated on these words with Fr. Peyton often and they transformed my faith. Praying the Rosary "has the power to capture God's attention."[6] I believed his words with all my heart and knew that the intercessory prayers of the Rosary were the source of many miracles in my own family.

The family Rosary also proved to be the source of deeper conversion and love of God.

One day, I found myself still struggling to be at peace with God's call for me to leave my work. I was praying in the quiet of the early morning when I heard Jesus whisper to me, "I know it was hard for you to leave

---

5   Ibid., 229.

6   Family Rosary, Father Patrick Peyton C.S.C., "*The Impassioned Apostle*", Oct 20, 2024, https://youtu.be/_5RKhBfuQbg?si=CSY-Xm6Gbb-2Q8w8.

the work that you loved, but can you see now that it was an answer to your family prayer? It was an answer to *her* prayer." And I knew instantly that the little girl who was the center of our family prayer had prayed for more time with her mama. I had been working and traveling since she was six years old. She was now starting high school, struggling to fit in, and questioning her faith like many girls her age.

Thinking back to the day when I felt those shackles falling from me as I left Fr. Peyton's room, I realized it was an answer to the prayer of a child who believed. Jesus had freed me to live out my primary vocation as a wife and mother. I was moved to tears and filled with a deep sense of gratitude for the miracle I didn't even know I needed.

All of the belongings from Fr Peyton's room have long since been moved from California to the Museum of Family Prayer just outside of Boston. As Fr. Peyton's self-proclaimed biggest fan, I made a trip there to pray at his grave, which coincided with moving my youngest daughter into her college dorm in Boston. After praying with Fr. Peyton, I felt at peace leaving her in this big city, 3,000 miles from home. I knew he would be watching over her.

I still pray with my favorite blue plastic rosary that was a gift from the Little Sisters. When they gave it to me, they shared that it had been blessed by Fr. Peyton before he died. Every once in a while, he still sends me a reminder that he is walking with me:

One morning I was planning to use the recorded voice of Fr. Peyton to pray with my rosary group. I wanted to be able to show them Fr. Peyton's picture and tell them about my favorite saint-to-be. As I brought up a photo of him onto my computer screen, above it in bold letters was his name: **FR. PEYTON.**

As soon as it flashed on my screen, tears flowed from my eyes. My first grandson was due any day, and the name my daughter and son-in-law had chosen was **PEYTON!**

Fr. Peyton's legacy of interceding for my family will be carried on in the daily reminder of my grandson bearing his name.

A holy moment helped me recognize that Fr. Peyton's intercession was multi-generational; from the prayers of my mother to me, and from me to my children and grandchildren. He was right, "The family rosary has saved the world in the past, and it will save the world now by saving the family."[7]

Through mentoring, speaking, and writing, **Christine Rich** is honored to walk with women navigating their earthly journey with God. Her passion for sharing about the power of prayer is modeled in her own life and drives her to form others in this gift she received from her own family and the family of the Catholic Church. Download the "Pray-Work-Live" printable booklet at *Archetype.Group/pray*

---

7   Jonathan Cipiti, *Pray: the Story of Patrick Peyton.* 2020, Family Theater Productions, Film/DVD.

XI

LIFE IN ABUNDANCE

How St. Thorlak Helped Me Appreciate
and Advocate for My Children

Mary Thissen

He sat across from me in the restaurant, arms folded, eyes averting mine. He leaned back in his chair and sighed, the toll of our conversation about his struggle with scrupulosity weighing heavy on him. Then the crux of the matter came out. He leaned in to speak, almost in a whisper. "I don't think the Church really cares about people like me," he said.

Those words pierced my heart. I knew that it wasn't true, but how could I acknowledge his anguish and suffering of living with autism while proving the Church really did care?

Later that evening I sat down with my tablet. I wasn't sure what I was looking for, but I wanted evidence that the Church cared for all of her children and that all were represented and loved even—*especially*—in their uniqueness.

Suddenly, a thought entered my head.

Of course, I thought to myself. The saints! There has to be a patron saint of neurodivergent people."

I took my tablet and searched for "patron saint of people with autism."

The first hit was someone I had never heard of: St. Thorlak.

As I read more about him, I was convinced that my friend needed to hear the story of St. Thorlak and of his monumental importance to the Church, even though most have never heard of him. Little did I know just how important he would become in my own life.

St. Thorlak Thorhallson was born in 1133 in Iceland. As a child, Thorlak was regarded as a prodigy—he taught himself to read and then memorized all 150 psalms. Ordained as a deacon at fifteen and a priest at eighteen, Thorlak was seen as not only a promising Church leader, but a political leader. Simony and lay patronage ran rampant in the Church in Iceland at that time, and it was expected that Thorlak would rise in prominence to keep the status quo. How wrong the leaders would be![1]

Thorlak became known for Church reforms in Iceland, primarily bringing churches and clergy under the law of the Church, without being funded or influenced by political leaders. Thorlak's efforts were made more difficult by Jon Loftsson, a leader who not only resisted Thorlak's efforts to reform the Church, but also was said to have carried on an extramarital affair with Thorlak's sister. Jon is even said to have put a hit on Thorlak's life by hiring someone to kill him with an ax. It is said that Thorlak made eye contact with the would-be assassin, who for some reason, became inexplicably paralyzed. Thorlak passed by the hitman and into the church unharmed.[2]

Thorlak was influenced by his time spent studying abroad. During this time, he came to know the Augustinians and was greatly influenced by their way of life. Later, he established Augustinian monasteries in Iceland. Thorlak preferred spending time with those considered "lesser" in society: the poor, the simple, and the disabled. This was not considered "becoming" of a person of such importance as he was. Thorlak was

---

1   Aimee O'Connell and Fr. Mark Nolette, "*St. Thorlak's Patronage to Autistic People*," Autism Consecrated, February 25, 2020, https://autismconsecrated.com/more-thorlak/.

2   Aimee O'Connell. *Thorlak of Iceland: Who Rose Above Autism to Become Patron Saint of His People* (San Jose, California: Chaos to Order Publishing, 2018).

often misunderstood. He had a passion for theology for which he could speak about for long periods of time, but often did not engage socially with others.

Today, we can look back on such "misunderstandings" and interpret them from a clinical standpoint. Thorlak was probably autistic, based on several factors, including failing to respond as expected to social interactions, an inflexible approach to routines and rituals, and possible speech impairment, as he was often reluctant to speak and only did so if absolutely necessary. These traits don't conclusively indicate autism. Rather, we can only speculate through the historical context that we have today.

The largest case for St. Thorlak's neurodiversity, however, may not come out of a clinical perspective, but a spiritual one. Neurodiverse people have indicated that, with St. Thorlak's intercession, they were able to make a major life decision, were led to their vocation, or simply felt affirmed that they, too, were members of the Body of Christ.[3] In this way, Thorlak leads us to the heart of Jesus, who came so that all "may have life, and have it more abundantly" (John 10:10).

St. Thorlak entered my life at a crucial point, before I gave birth to what I call my "miracle babies." I had had three miscarriages and an ectopic pregnancy before I welcomed twins. I thought the hard part was over when I finally had my babies, but I was wrong. By God's grace, Thorlak had already entered my life, standing by as a silent advocate for what was perhaps to be my hardest job yet: mother of neurodiverse children.

In a way, I myself related to St. Thorlak and could identify with parts of his story. Though I am not classified as a neurodiverse person, I felt on the fringes of the Catholic Church for so long that I felt as if I was the outcast Jesus so frequently referenced in His ministry. I saw happy, young, holy couples bringing children into the world with ease. My heart ached for what they had. My hopes were driven to the heights by each pregnancy,

---

3   Ibid, 208–209.

only to come crashing down in despair when I learned my pregnancies were not viable. I can only imagine Thorlak may have looked at others and wondered why he was so different from them. I looked at those around me and wondered the same.

When I was finally given the gift of two children here on earth, I knew motherhood wouldn't be a cakewalk, but I was not prepared for what I would hear from their doctor. Not only did one child seem to have problems with vision, both children were neurodiverse.

My heart sank.

Did I know, in my heart and soul, that these children were made in the image and likeness of God and were therefore exactly who God made them to be? Of this I had no doubt. Why my heart sank, what I grieved for, was the difficulty I knew they would have in life. The cruelty. The judgment. The whispers and snickers behind their backs. Being seen as different and unworthy because they experienced the world in a different way than some people think is acceptable.

Then, I recalled that initial encounter with St. Thorlak.

Gradually, subtly, slowly, I felt peace. I had absolutely no explanation for this peace. The only explanation for this peace was that it was of Jesus, through the intercession of St. Thorlak, guarding my heart and mind (Philippians 4:7).

Through Thorlak's example and help, I came to understand that each person has their unique place in the Body of Christ. My children were made as God intended for the specific call He has placed on their lives. As a believer in and follower of Jesus, I always knew this in an intellectual sense, but as the saying goes, the longest journey one will ever take is from the head to the heart. Realizing this, I asked myself, *Is my faith only intellectual? Or do I know with my whole being that God exists, Jesus walked among us on earth, died, and rose on the third day, and has sent the Holy Spirit among us as the Advocate?* And so, after the despair of my four previous lost pregnancies, my faith deepened and strengthened. I could feel myself deepening and stretching and growing in faith, even when I didn't understand how tomorrow would look, much less the next eighteen or so years.

For centuries, Thorlak has been a hero of the Icelandic people. He was unofficially declared a saint in Iceland and in the Lutheran church in Iceland, but he remained primarily only known and loved in Iceland until recent times, when St. John Paul II canonized him in the Catholic Church in 1984.[4]

Thorlak died in 1193, when the concepts of neurodiversity or autism hadn't been conceptualized. I believe it is by God's provident design that Thorlak was canonized in the 1980s in the Catholic Church just as such research and knowledge began to gain traction around the world. As a society, we began to deepen our understanding of those who were different from us. Neurodiverse persons were beginning to understand who they were, and in turn, we began to identify and exemplify persons throughout history who were most likely neurodivergent. Thorlak, then, can stand as an example for all of the Christian faithful who are called neurodivergent.

I don't believe Thorlak was canonized just to intercede for those who are neurodivergent; I believe he intercedes for parents, siblings, friends, and all loved ones of neurodivergent people. I know he interceded for me before I even knew I needed him. I know I can continue to ask him to pray to God for me regarding any aspect of my children's life: physical or medical, educational, psychological or spiritual. Thorlak is here for me as a mother and advocate for my children. Our Communion of Saints, then, can be called active and dynamic in our world; they are not static, historical figures, but living in glory that no eye has seen, no ear has heard (1 Corinthians 2:9).

Finally, I know Thorlak accompanies our family on the journey of life. Since my children are so young, how their lives will play out remains to be seen. I can let that fill me with fear, or I can turn to the incredible

---

4   Ibid, xiii.

example of merciful love and compassion that Thorlak brought to his people. I often think about Thorlak living in twelfth-century Iceland, growing up, perhaps not quite understanding why he was different or how his particular gifts would be used for good.

I also think of Thorlak's mother, of what she must have gone through and asked God for her son. I wonder if she felt it all: confusion, sadness, even anger that her child was "different." When I think of her, I have more compassion and understanding for myself. On days when the appointments, the therapies, the sensory meltdowns all feel too much, I ask for Thorlak's intercession to make the best choice I can for my children and for the strength and peace that first came to me when I heard Thorlak's story. I then ask for it again when I feel all of the roller coaster of emotions that come with being a special-needs parent. If Thorlak was able to live in such times that autism had not yet been identified, I can certainly be a physical and spiritual force for good for my children, having insight and medical and practical resources not previously in existence. We know not what tomorrow brings, but in the love of Jesus, we are cared for no matter what.

Prayer to St. Thorlak

St. Thorlak, intercede for all persons who are neurodivergent. May they know their place in the Body of Christ and their ability to make an impact on the world. Keep them, their family, and their friends close to Jesus, and remind them that they are made perfect in the image and likeness of God. Amen.

Mary Thissen writes about knowing and loving God through adversity, including her own experiences of pregnancy loss and special-needs parenthood. She desires that all know who have been given these crosses that they are capable, strong, and loved by the Lord. Find out more about her and her writing at *marythissen.com*.

XII

BEHOLD THY MOTHER

How the Queen of Peace Took Me
Deeper into the Heart of Jesus

Brenda Kostial

A s I walked a winding path through my backyard while praying the Rosary with my friend over the phone, I suddenly stopped and stood beneath the old oak, blurting out in the middle of a Hail Mary, "I want to go to Medjugorje!" Those words were immediately followed by the thought: *I have to pack up my classroom!* I stared into the evening sky through the branches above me in awe, crying tears of consolation as the love of the Blessed Mother flooded over me from above.

I felt her. I finally felt her!

This intimacy is what had been missing when I prayed "As I Kneel"[1] each day! Some time before, I had begun to pray the lyrics of this beautiful song to Our Lady, but when I prayed the last lines about seeing "her smiling face"[2] and my thoughts being "lost in her embrace,"[3] they hadn't

---

1 Eliott Yozwiak. "'As I Kneel before You' with Lyrics | AirMaria.com." AirMaria.com | Breathe Freely. April 30, 2018. https://airmaria.com/2018/04/30/as-i-kneel-before-you-with-lyrics/.

2 Ibid.

3 Ibid.

felt true. Now I stood in wonder, wrapped in her embrace in the way I had so deeply desired.

In those few moments of encounter with the love of Our Lady during her most holy Rosary, I knew I was going to Medjugorje and knew that it would be very soon, because I blurted out those life-changing words on May 24, on the Feast of Mary, Mother of the Church. And the last day of school was in only eleven days!

I have a Heavenly Mother who holds me tenderly in her heart and who desires to take me deeper into the Heart of Her Son, Jesus. She is your Mother, too. She is Mother of us all, for she is Mother of the Church, given by her Son as she stood at the foot of His Cross, "Behold, thy Mother" (John 19:26–27).

My Mother had called me to go to her in Medjugorje, where she tells her children, "If you knew how much I love you, you'd cry with joy."[4]

St. Elizabeth, the mother of John the Baptist, asked, "And how does this happen to me, that the mother of my Lord should come to me?" (Luke 1:43). We may also find ourselves asking why Our Lady would come to us. This Scripture often wells up within me, bringing me to tears. She comes because she is our Mother. A mother teaches her children through her presence, through a heart to heart personal relationship.[5] Our Lady comes to be present with her children and to teach them the way of her Son.

Since 1981 the Blessed Mother has come as the Queen of Peace to the small village of Medjugorje in southern Bosnia-Herzegovina, where the Franciscans brought and preserved the Catholic faith, many with their martyrdom, for the region was under a Communist regime when Our Lady first appeared on June 24, 1981. On the Feast of St. John the Baptist,

---

4   June 21, 1984 to Jelena Vasilj "Messages 1981-2023." 2023. Medjugorje.org. 2023. https://www.medjugorje.org/messagesall.htm.

5   St. Peter Julian Eymard. *The Real Presence*. Edited by Paul A. Boer, Sr. (Veritatis Splendor Publications, 2013), 195.

Ivanka, the first visionary to see Our Lady on the Hill of Apparitions, exclaimed, "I think I see Our Lady on the hill!"[6]

Her friend Mirjana's response was doubtful. "Yeah, sure it's Our Lady! She came to see what the two of us are up to because she has nothing better to do!"[7] Mirjana, a teenager from Sarajevo who spent summers with her aunt and uncle in Medjugorje,[8] had never heard of apparitions such as Fatima or Lourdes. She thought the Blessed Mother would be in Heaven.[9] The next day, Mirjana experienced the reality of the Blessed Mother who seemed to bring heaven with her when she appeared to them, and she didn't want the apparition to end.[10]

Forty-three years after the first apparition, Ivan spoke publicly of how he had asked the Blessed Mother, "Why me?" She told him she doesn't choose the best ones. She chose these humble children.

> *"Dear children, this is the reason for my presence among you for such a long time: to lead you on the path of Jesus. I want to save you and, through you, to save the whole world"* (July 30, 1987).[11]

The Queen of Peace calls us to conversion, to teach us the way of peace through prayer from the heart, asking us to decide for God and live her messages as apostles of her love. She asks for our prayers and sacrifices so that God's plans can be accomplished through her, changing the world one heart at a time to bring about the Triumph of her Immaculate Heart.

Father Leon Pereira, Chaplain to the English-speaking pilgrims in Medjugorje, speaks of his encounter with the Blessed Mother. When he asked her who she was, she said, "I am your mother, the Mother of God.

6   Mirjana Soldo, Sean Bloomfield, and Miki Musa. *My Heart Will Triumph* (2016), 12.
7   Ibid., 12.
8   Ibid., 6.
9   Ibid., 16.
10 Ibid., 30.
11 "Medjugorje-Our Lady Queen of Peace." In Defense of the Cross. April 2, 2020. https://indefenseofthecross.com/marian-apparitions/medjugorje-our-lady/.

I want you to tell everyone that you meet that I am their mother and that I love them." He continued, "It's no use fighting her. She loves you."[12]

Our Lady called me to Medjugorje so that I would know that she is my Mother. And that she loves me.

I answered Our Lady's call. Snjezana, my pilgrim guide, took me first to the statue of Our Lady at St. James Church.

I climbed Mt. Krizevac, stepping from one large footworn rock to another on the rugged steep path, stopping to pray at each Station of the Cross, and offering my crosses to our Lord at the station of His Crucifixion. I prayed at the foot of the massive cross erected in 1933 by villagers whose faith moved them to commemorate the Crucifixion of Christ. Grace and peace swept over me as I gazed upon the village and St. James Church on the plain below.

I witnessed humility, trust, and a great act of love when men from the Cenacolo Community carried a terminally ill man in a pole chair up the slippery rocks of Apparition Hill in the rain, stopping at each of the mysteries as we prayed the Rosary in Italian. Seeing the ill man's gratitude as he reached Our Lady's statue and hearing the conversion stories of the men from the community deeply touched my heart.

I walked to St. James Church with pilgrims and villagers for the incredibly beautiful evening prayer program. Long lines formed for confessions even with so many priests seated along the church wall and in the confessionals. I expressed my surprise to the local woman in front of me that the priest would take so long when so many others were waiting. She patiently replied that perhaps this man had not been to confession for a very long time and needed that time with the priest. Later I recognized this as my first lesson in Medjugorje—the need to grow in humility and love.

I knelt before one of the myriad benches that fan out from the altar to seat the thousands of people gathering to pray the Rosary and the Holy Mass, with prayer from the heart out of love of God and reverence for the

---

12 Heard personally during Father Leon's talk to the English pilgrims in June of 2021 and 2024.

Most Blessed Sacrament. At 5:40 p.m. the Rosary paused, and all waited in silence as the Blessed Mother appeared to Marija, Ivan, and Vicka.

Heaven came to earth.

There was grace in this place, and a profound peace settled over me and the praying parish.

After several minutes, the Rosary resumed, followed by the Holy Mass and either reverent Adoration of the Blessed Sacrament or the Glorious Mysteries. Finally, after the concluding prayers, the outdoor nave slowly began to empty.

I didn't want to leave the peace of Medjugorje. I brought home many memories, including the night that Snjezana took me to meet Marija and to be present in her chapel for one of the apparitions, which brought such grace. I brought five stones from Apparition Hill to represent what Father Jozo calls the "Five Stones," the five main ideas of Our Lady's messages.[13]

Most importantly, I brought with me the desire to be more like my Mother.

St. John Paul II's devotion to the Blessed Mother was at the heart of his papacy. When he lost his own mother at the age of nine, his father took him to a Marian Shrine, telling him, "From today on she will be your mother."[14] Although he couldn't go to Medjugorje while he was pope, since the apparitions were not yet approved, his show of support was clear in his conversations with those close to him.[15] He called Medjugorje "the spiritual heart of the world,"[16] telling Italian scientists investigating the apparitions, "Today's world has lost its sense of the supernatural, but many are searching

---

13 Father Jozo Zovko. 2008. *Called to Love*. Stroki Brijeg: International Godparenthood for the Herzeg-Bosnian Child.

14 "Wojtyła's Father Entrusted Karol to Our Lady: 'from Today on She Will Be Your Mother.'" n.d. Aleteia—Catholic Spirituality, Lifestyle, World News, and Culture. https://aleteia. org/2021/05/09/wojtylas-father-entrusted-karol-to-our-lady-from-today-on-she-will-be-your-mother.

15 "Pope John Paul II 'Medjugorje – the Spiritual Heart of the World.'" Medjugorje.org. 2015. https://www.medjugorje.org/wordpress/archives/33.

16 Ibid.

for it and find it in Medjugorje, through prayer, penance, and fasting." [17] He acknowledged the visionaries when he saw them in Rome and told Mirjana in a personal meeting, "Medjugorje is the hope for the entire world."[18]

The Church has acknowledged that the spiritual fruits of Medjugorje are many, especially conversions and vocations. On September 19, 2024, the Nihil obstat was given to the spiritual experience of Medjugorje by the Dicastery for the Doctrine of the Faith.[19]

The Queen of Peace calls us and then sends us forth so that all her children might come to know the love of God.

The fruit of my pilgrimage unfolded two months later, on the Feast of the Assumption, when I scanned the church bulletin and saw that my parish's school was looking for a teacher. Thoughts about my longtime public school teaching position first filled my mind. Then I felt the stirring of the Holy Spirit, and the tears of consolation came.

I remembered a signal grace! The day I had left for my pilgrimage, a book that had been gifted to me had arrived, *Fatima Mysteries: Mary's Messages for the Modern Age.*

And the name of the school with the open position? Our Lady of Fatima.

I smiled through my sobs, knowing as I had with my pilgrimage that I was to take this position. Our Lady was calling me to Catholic education to freely share her love and her Son with my students!

A year later, our Lord and Our Lady moved me to a different Catholic school, guiding me with clear signal graces to a position I now hold that wasn't available the previous year. Then, the following year, again on the Feast of Mary, Mother of the Church, Our Lady called me to write. As it is written on my heart, I will write it down.

---

17 Ibid.

18 "Pope John Paul II 'Medjugorje – the Spiritual Heart of the World.'" Medjugorje.org. 2015. https://www.medjugorje.org/wordpress/archives/33.

19 "'The Queen of Peace': Note about the Spiritual Experience Connected with Medjugorje (19 September 2024)." https://www.vatican.va/roman_curia/congregations/cfaith/documents/rc_ddf_doc_20240919_nota-esperienza-medjugorje_en.html.

Three years after my pilgrimage, I returned to Medjugorje. God had more to do in my heart, and although it surprised me, my Mother knew, and she was with me on Cross Mountain.

From Medjugorje I went to Italy and to the Holy House of Loreto, removing my sandals as I entered, touching the stone walls of the house where the Angel Gabriel came to the Virgin of Nazareth, where Our Lady said, "May it be done to me according to your word" (Luke 1:38). She invites us to give our own fiat to our Lord.

From Loreto, I went to Assisi, where St. Francis converted, gave up everything to follow Jesus, and lived a life of poverty and penance after an encounter with our Lord and a vision of Lady Poverty. Francis was filled with inexplicable joy that moved many others to conversion, including St. Clare, who also gave up everything to follow our Lord. Conversion begets conversion.

The reward of a life lived for Jesus is profound intimacy, for our hearts were made for God. Our Mother knows this and wants all of her children to turn to God, to be with her in heaven.

I invite you to a personal relationship with Our Lady, to intimacy with Jesus through Mary. Come to her simply, as a little child with an open heart, and speak to her as your "most beloved mother."[20]

Ask her, as St. Mother Theresa did, "Mary, Mother of Jesus, please be a mother to me now."[21]

Pray, *"Take this day, make it yours, and fill me with your love."*[22]

She will respond, for she is your Mother, and she loves you.

Our Lady, Queen of Peace and Our Mother, pray for us!

---

20 Second Vatican Council, "Dogmatic Constitution on the Church, *Lumen gentium*, 21 November, 1964," in *Vatican Council II: The Conciliar and Post Conciliar Documents*, ed. Austin Flannery (Collegeville, MN: Liturgical Press, 1975), sec. 53 (hereafter cited as *LG*).

21 Rita Buettner. "Mary, Be a Mother to Me Now - Catholic Review." May 5, 2022. https://catholicreview.org/mary-be-a-mother-to-me-now/.

22 Eliott Yozwiak. "'As I Kneel before You' with Lyrics | AirMaria.com." AirMaria.com | Breathe Freely. April 30, 2018. https://airmaria.com/2018/04/30/as-i-kneel-before-you-with-lyrics/.

Brenda Kostial writes to invite readers to deeper surrender and intimacy with God, entrusting all to Jesus through our Blessed Mother. A teacher, writer, and speaker, she loves sharing her witness of the peace, joy, wonder, and awe of a life lived for Jesus. Learn more and download printable copies of Consecration Prayers given by Our Lady at *brendakostial.com*.

XIII

THE DOOR TO MY HEART

How Blessed Solanus Casey Continues
to Intercede for My Healing

Carolyn Lauman

Alongside my fellow parishioners, I pulled cartons of microwavable mac and cheese from the pantry shelf, then wedged them into paper sacks already overflowing with cans of chunky soup and green beans, jars of peanut butter and tomato sauce, boxes of cereal and pasta, sleeves of crackers, and single rolls of toilet paper. The grocery bags were bulging, almost too heavy to carry, but the needy souls who rang our doorbell would be hungry, and the food was available only one morning a week.

Under the auspices of the St. Vincent de Paul Society, our parish food pantry operates from Labor Day through Memorial Day, when the restaurants, hotels, and other tourism-related businesses in our beach town are shut down. During this off-season, furloughed employees have the option to accept temporary employment elsewhere or to apply for government-sponsored unemployment benefits. Some, however, do not or cannot take advantage of either option, which is where we come in.

Among those who do not or cannot are the increasing number of immigrants who, unfamiliar with our language and the complicated labyrinth of rules and regulations, fall through the available government safety nets. Proud but vulnerable, they arrive at our door to inquire about ESL (English as a Second Language) classes and to pick up a much-needed bag of groceries.

As I rolled the cart of bags into the foyer of the parish hall, I comforted myself with the knowledge that the food we distributed wasn't meant to meet the totality of a recipient's needs but lend a *temporary* helping hand. Other churches and charities in our small coastal community also provided assistance, including shelter for the homeless, so I didn't need to be concerned that our tiny operation wasn't serving all those in need.

By the time the pantry closed down for the day, we had distributed ten bags of food, including one to a woman, who was neither working nor receiving assistance from state or federal agencies and was feeding a household of six. She had graciously accepted what little we offered, but I silently questioned how her family would make it through the week, let alone the winter.

I left the parish hall troubled by an uneasiness that prodded my conscience. The nagging disquiet was in no way associated with the people we had served, but rather with the desperate situation in which they found themselves. New to the pantry, I had been largely oblivious to the privations of many of those residing in our community, and while I was now doing something to help, it hardly seemed enough.

Beside my car, the noonday sun glinted off an object lying in the grassy median. With a gasp, I recognized the small plastic badge that held a photo and tiny relic of Blessed Solanus Casey, through whose intercession in October 2020 I had been graced with the favor of sobriety. The relic must have slipped from the biography I had brought to read during quiet moments. I quickly picked up the lightweight medallion and pressed it to my chest. Glancing skyward, I thanked God that my treasured relic hadn't blown away in the ever-present coastal breeze.

During his lifetime, Father Solanus Casey was well-known as a healer and "holy priest." Now on track for sainthood, Blessed Solanus Casey continues to be so much more than a miracle worker.

Ordained in 1904 as a simplex priest, the bearded and bespectacled Capuchin friar was not permitted to hear confessions nor grant absolution, but those who sought him out for healing, consolation, advice, and prayer were largely undeterred by these limitations. Whether assigned to a parish in Brooklyn, New York, or working as a porter at his monastery in Detroit, Michigan, or confined to a hospital bed while being treated for a persistent skin disease, thousands upon thousands of people knocked at his door. With unwavering love and compassion, he welcomed everyone, no matter their faith, often spending time he didn't have to simply listen.

Likewise, as a founder of the soup kitchen at the Capuchin Monastery of St. Bonaventure in Detroit, he personified the role of the good shepherd, fulfilling Jesus's mandate to Peter in John 21:17 to "feed my sheep." Unlike my own parish's weekly food pantry, the Capuchin soup kitchen served upwards of three thousand people every single day during the Great Depression of the 1930s. To this day, it is one of the largest, if not the largest, of the private charities in Michigan.[1]

Father Solanus treated the downtrodden who frequented the soup kitchen with the utmost dignity and respect. He truly believed that "the poor have as much right to the food as we." When the daily crowds became unmanageable for the Capuchin friars alone to feed, Solanus asked those who sought his favor to show their gratitude by performing a corporal work of mercy for the kitchen.[2]

> What a marvelously different society we would have here and what an ideal world we would have to live in if we all would keep in mind the assurance of Jesus, 'What you have done to the least of my brethren, *you have done to me.*'[3]

---

1   Fr. Ed Foley, from the video documentary *They Might Be Saints: Blessed Solanus Casey* (EWTN, 2021), viewed on SolanusCasey.org.
2   Michael Crosby, OFM Cap., *Thank God Ahead of Time: The Life and Spirituality of Solanus Casey* (Cincinnati: Franciscan Media, 2009), 107.
3   Solanus Casey in a letter to Mrs. Geraci, c 1947, as found in *Thank God Ahead of Time*, 173.

Though elated to have recovered my relic, my sense of unease remained. With the aim of examining that feeling through a Christ-centered lens—something I had been encouraged to practice at my silent retreat on Ignatian spirituality the weekend before—I began to dig a little deeper.

In the retreat's opening session, our wise and witty master, a priest with the Legionaries of Christ, likened a personal retreat to a door that Jesus wishes to enter. He encouraged us to meditate on Jesus, who stands at the door to our hearts. With gifts in hand, He knocks gently but persistently, beckoning to come in.

"Behold, I stand at the door and knock; if any one hears my voice and opens the door, I will come in to him and eat with him, and he with me" *(Revelation 3:20).*

This meditation resonated strongly with me, so much so, as I knelt in the chapel that first evening, I felt a physical tightness in my chest, as if my heart were enclosed within a clenched fist.

The next day, as I journaled in my modest bedroom, the Holy Spirit prompted me to draw a door centered on a wall. Using my limited talent of perspective drawing, my efforts revealed a door that was slightly ajar, the opening not quite wide enough to permit anything of size to pass through.

As I stayed with the meditation over the weekend, I began to visualize my heart encased within a thick wall—a wall that I, myself, constructed. Like my drawing, a door allows access through the outer wall, but more often than not I keep it closed tightly and locked. While I am able to envision myself living a freer, more joyful existence, I justify the wall and its locked door because they keep my heart safe. *Better to live a "less-than" life than to expose my vulnerability to others. Better to protect myself from an influx of pain, rejection, and loss than to open myself to something—or someone—better.*

Sadly, my intractable fear has done nothing more than prevent me from experiencing the beautiful life I was created to live, a life overflowing with every good gift from Jesus—far greater gifts than the ones I already possess and selfishly hoard, like the gift of sobriety received through the intercession of Blessed Solanus Casey after I trustingly opened my heart to the possibility that I could be healed.

Ever humble, Blessed Solanus refused to accept accolades for the favors received through his intercession. When grateful recipients wished to honor him in some fashion, he insisted that all glory was God's alone. Rather than acknowledge his own role in a healing, he credited the prayers that were prayed, the Mass that was said, or the works of charity done in thanksgiving.[4]

> "Beware of practicing your piety before men in order to be seen by them: for then you will have no reward from your Father who is in heaven. Thus, when you give alms, sound no trumpet before you, as the hypocrites do in the synagogues and in the streets, that they may be praised by men. Truly, I say to you, they have their reward. But when you give alms, do not let your left hand know what your right hand is doing, so that your alms may be in secret; and your Father who sees in secret will reward you" (Matthew 6:1–4).

These truths came flooding back to me as I drove from the church parking lot. Patient though he is, I suspected Blessed Solanus had grown weary of waiting for me to promise "a little sacrifice of some kind in thanksgiving."[5] With the approach of the fourth anniversary of my sobriety, the time had long passed to offer corporal works of mercy in imitation of Jesus, who has been knocking, gently but persistently, at my heart's door. It was time for me to feed His sheep, as St. Peter did, and as Solanus did so faithfully on earth, and does to this very day from heaven. And to think when my day had begun, I was feeling rather pleased with myself for sacrificing one lowly morning each month. *OK, OK,* I responded. *I'll look into what more I can do.*

---

4   Michael Crosby, OFM Cap., *Thank God Ahead of Time: The Life and Spirituality of Solanus Casey* (Cincinnati: Franciscan Media, 2009), 56.

5   Ibid., 164.

Two days later, as I sat typing on my laptop, an email popped up on my screen. The president of the St. Vincent de Paul Society was asking for additional help with the food pantry. Could someone volunteer a little time and effort to assist with the shopping and stocking? Without weighing the pros and cons *ad infinitum* as I was previously wont to do, I replied with a yes, I can. Yes, I will. "A new heart I will give you, and a new spirit I will put within you; and I will remove from your flesh the heart of stone and give you a heart of flesh" (Ezekiel 36:26).

Surely, there is still more I can do, more I should do, but I have been blessed with a greater appreciation for the blessings I have been given, especially the understanding that my earthly life isn't about me alone. Jesus has always known this, which is why He willingly suffered and died for each and every one of the children His Father entrusted to His care. Blessed Solanus knows this, interceding still for the thousands of children God has entrusted to him. And as Blessed Solanus was fond of saying, I shall forever "thank God ahead of time" for whomever He entrusts to my care.

Through the widening doorway to my inner heart, I can sense a new blessing taking root. Not the favor of an outwardly visible healing, but a healing, nonetheless. The stone of stubborn selfishness has been excavated, and in its place, a tiny bud of compassion has been sown. In time, the weeds of fear will be overtaken by vibrant bouquets of hope. I look forward to sharing each and every blossom.

Prayer for the Canonization of Blessed Solanus Casey

O God, I adore You. I give myself to You.
May I be the person You want me to be,
and may Your will be done in my life today.
I thank You for the gifts You gave Father Solanus.
If it is Your Will, bless us with the Canonization of
Father Solanus so that others may imitate and carry on his love
For all the poor and suffering of our world.
As he joyfully accepted Your divine plans,
I ask You, according to Your will,
To hear my prayer for... (your intention)
Through Jesus Christ our Lord. Amen.
"Blessed be God in all His Designs."

Imprimatur
+Most Reverend Allen H. Vigneron
Archbishop of Detroit

Carolyn Courtney Lauman writes for the purpose and glory of God. Blessed with a healing favor through the intercession of Blessed Solanus Casey, she is inspired to share her salvation and faith with others needing encouragement to come home to the Catholic Church. You can read more of Carolyn's works at *HisResurrectionFern.com.*

XIV

A Mother's Tears

How St. Monica Helped Me Release the "If Onlys"

Margaret Gartlgruber

I really hate when I cry in public, especially at church. But there I was, alone at Sunday Mass. I felt such sorrow that tears just spilled out, no matter how hard I fought them.

Why didn't I bring any tissues? I used the inside of my sleeve, attempting to hide the fact that I was wiping my nose. I was certain everyone was staring at me, wondering what awful thing had happened to cause the tears. *Nothing, really. I am OK!* I wanted to tell them. I was just alone.

I wondered where I had gone wrong. I had four children and one simple mission: raise my kids to get to heaven. At least I thought it was simple enough. I thought I had done everything I was supposed to do. I took them to church every Sunday, I taught their CCD classes, I prayed with them, read to them, taught them all things I was sure would have helped me when I was young. Yet, now that they were older, I realized I had failed, and the world, it seemed, had succeeded. Not a single one of them was attending Mass. The reality of this failure hit me hard on that particular Sunday.

Continuing with my self pity, I proceeded to go through my *"Litany of If Only"*:

If only we had prayed more.
If only we had attended daily Mass more.
If only we had homeschooled.
If only we'd had enough money for Catholic school.
If only we lived in a more vibrant Catholic community.

"If only" any of these things, maybe I would not be alone today.

I looked up, contemplating Jesus on the Cross, imploring him for help. I looked to Mary and Joseph, begging for their intercession. Finally, I looked around me in the congregation and saw many strong faithful women, also alone, and I wondered about their families. Where were they? As my mind continued to wander, I remembered several strong Christian families, who had actually done all of the things I had not done, and yet they had literally lost their children to worldly values in much worse ways than I had. Was no one exempt?

My thoughts eventually turned to St. Monica, someone else who had cried about a child leaving the faith. The patron saint of mothers of wayward children, St. Monica is most known for praying and weeping for the conversion of her son, Augustine, for seventeen years. Born in the year 329, St. Monica's story could be told today: a Christian girl in a difficult marriage with an unfaithful, verbally abusive pagan husband, an equally difficult mother-in-law, and a wayward child given to the ways of the world instead of God.

Remarkably, Monica prayed for her husband, and he converted. She prayed for her mother-in-law, and she converted. She prayed for her son, and he converted.

Looking again at Christ on the Cross, I prayed: *Lord, I understand that we need to persevere in prayer like St. Monica, but I would like to remind you that I actually have been praying for my children about as long as she did. Is it not time for you to do your magic and convert them?*

In response, something niggled at my brain—a story my spiritual director told me about how St. Monica almost stopped her son, Augustine, from getting on a ship that eventually led to his conversion. Feeling challenged to go deeper into St. Monica's life, I opened up *Confessions of St. Augustine* to find the details for myself. I was surprised to learn that Monica's was a story about a lot more than just weeping and praying. Her story was about action and staying still ... about persistence and patience ... about acceptance of others and examination of self.

Ultimately, it was about pride and surrender.

Monica was in such anguish, loathing the choices her son was making against God, she found it difficult to even be around him and was on the verge of kicking him from their home

God, hearing her cries and seeing the puddles of tears pouring from her eyes drenching the ground in all of the areas she prayed, came to her in a dream to console her. He urged her to look at herself standing on the "wooden ruler" with her son next to her on that same ruler.

Comforted by this vision from God, Monica reconciled her relationship with Augustine, allowing him to live with her. When she told him of her dream, Augustine argued the meaning, "You see, you will soon come around and be with me." She smiled a knowing smile, telling him, "No, no—what was said to me wasn't 'Where he is you are too,' but 'Where you are, he is too.'"[1]

Monica realized that by staying close to her son, standing firm in the faith, and never ceasing to weep for him for eight more years, would be the best way to show him God.

As Augustine entered adulthood, he became immersed in the Manichaean heresy. Nothing Monica said or did would persuade him away from it. While continuing to weep and pray, she discovered her local

---

1   St. Augustine, *Confessions*. Translated by Sarah Ruden (New York: Random House, 2017), 71–72.

bishop had also been involved in this same heresy, yet had converted to the Catholic Faith.

Thinking this was the person to help her, Monica began a campaign of persuasion for this bishop to talk her son out of his mistaken ideas.

Her request did not go as she expected, since try as she might, the bishop declined, saying, "He is not going to listen to me. He is not yet teachable. Leave him alone."

A relentless Monica would not stop weeping while begging and pleading. She annoyed him so much, he finally said, "Get out of here." When the bishop saw her tears spilling in earnest, he was filled with pity for this poor mother, and said, *Just go on living this way. It's impossible that the son of these tears should perish."*

"Like thunder from heaven,"[2] she felt comforted and satisfied as she left the bishop, certain that God had spoken to her through him.

Monica's fearlessness, boldness, and persistence won her the consolation from God of knowing that her tears were not wasted and that her son would be saved.

Later, Augustine insisted that he would go to Rome to advance his career. He was very good at speaking and his talents were highly sought-after. Monica had other ideas, however. Determined to keep him from boarding the ship to Rome and the perils involved, she followed him to the sea, continuing to pester him to stay home. Augustine realized the only way he would escape her was deceit, so he lied and told her the voyage had been delayed. Persuading her to go to her room to sleep, he boarded the ship.[3]

Monica, in her determination to keep him safe, almost kept him from taking the voyage that changed his life forever. At the end of the voyage, which eventually landed him in Milan, he met Bishop Ambrose. This meeting was instrumental in his eventual conversion.

---

2   Ibid, 73–74.

3   Ibid, 121.

Of course, Monica would not sit quietly by. She embarked on the very dangerous journey herself, following him until she finally caught up with him in Milan. Upon her arrival, she discovered that her son had relinquished his heretical ideas. While still not a Catholic, he was finally listening to someone of knowledge in the faith—Bishop Ambrose (later to become St. Ambrose).

After Bishop Ambrose became Monica's spiritual director, she began focusing more on purification of her own soul and recognizing her own limitations.[4]

Several years later, Monica finally witnessed her son's baptism, and her mission was thus completed! Not long after, Monica fell ill and died.

Although her mission was over, God's was just beginning. Augustine not only became a priest, but also the Bishop of Hippo, and later, one of the greatest of saints (and a Doctor) of the Church.

+++

In today's society, some might say that Monica was a "helicopter parent," hovering around her child, controlling his movements in an effort to keep him from harm. Others may see her as lamenting and praying in church for hours on end without taking action. The reality is, Monica's story is far more complex. Her story is one of both action and prayer, of temptations to control and invitations to surrender, of loving, letting go, and letting God be God.

Seeing Monica struggle with the idea of kicking Augustine out of her house but then submitting by allowing him to stay shows us how to stand firm in our own faith and at the same time maintain a relationship with our loved ones, despite their chosen lifestyles. When worldviews start coming out of closets, we can refuse to hide in one. We can allow others the freedom and space to find their way to God, while refusing to hide or change our beliefs for fear of losing someone we love. Maybe the faith

4   Ibid, 134–136.

example we set makes all the difference! "Let your light so shine before men, that they may see your good works and give glory to your Father who is in heaven" (Matthew 5:16).

Seeing Moncia badger her bishop to talk Augustine out of his beliefs shows that we are not alone! We must be willing to seek help from others to help our children, even if it means we are annoying, as the widow who kept bothering the judge: "Because this widow bothers me, I will vindicate her" (Luke 18:5).

Seeing Monica being told that her son was not teachable shows that sometimes we need to back off from our own children, recognize that some things they need to figure out for themselves, that they are not willing to hear us, and that we need to practice patience and perseverance.

Seeing Monica chase her son to prevent him from taking a dangerous journey, then Augustine deceiving her only to go behind her back, and finally Monica following him on that dangerous journey herself shows us to be bold when our children face danger with certain choices.

Monica shows us that we must, at times, allow our children to board their own "ships," trusting in God's love for them, prayerfully following that ship, reminding them who they are and where they come from, seeking the bigger picture that only God sees and opening our imagination to the wonderful way God will work to grant better things for our children. "For I know the plans I have for you, says the Lord, plans for welfare and not for evil, to give you a future and a hope" (Jeremiah 29:11).

Finally, seeing Monica's continuous weeping shows it is through our prayer and tears for our children that we, ourselves, can be purified. We must remember that our children are God's children, and while we cooperate in raising them, only He can be their Savior, which can liberate us from fear and paralysis—and a lot of "what ifs."

This new way of seeing Monica, a woman of contradictions and conflicting desires—and yet ultimately a saint—gave me a new way to view myself. No longer could I be hard on myself or consider myself a failure. I now recognize the power of a mother's tears, seeing a road that may be filled with sorrow, suffering, and struggle. I resolve to release these tears and let them flow freely and unashamedly, wetting the ground wherever I pray.

Even at Sunday Mass. When I am alone. And when I've forgotten my tissues.

Looking back at my Litany of "If Only," I realized what was missing: Jesus. My litany was filled with things that *I* should have done differently. I left God out of it. I left prayer out of it. I made it all about me lamenting past actions.

Here is my new litany! I will focus on the present, asking that St. Monica, St. Augustine, and St. Ambrose intercede for me, to help me grow in the ways of St. Monica's witness.

Litany of St. Monica, St. Augustine, and St. Ambrose

Lord please hear this prayer!

To pray unceasingly for my loved ones
Pray for me!

To weep unashamedly for my loved ones
Pray for me!

To love unconditionally
Pray for me!

To root out sin keeping me from God
Pray for me!

To live strong and unwavering in my Faith
Pray for me!

To stay silent when needed
Pray for me!

To cooperate in God's will, even if I do not understand it
Pray for me!

To not put limits on God
Pray for me!

To show Jesus to all who know me through my words and actions
Pray for me!

Amen.

Margaret Gartlgruber longs for moms to know how important their call to motherhood is and that they are more than enough! As a semi-retired stay-at-home mom, Margaret writes of her experiences, strengths and hopes in Catholic family life hoping to encourage young moms to embrace their vocation. Find out more and get your free copy of *15 Simple Morning Prayers* at *ruledbybananas.com*.

XV

THE APOSTLE OF CHARITY

How St. Vincent de Paul Helped Me Find
My Hidden Role in the Body of Christ

Charlene Unterkofler

With a desperately pounding heart, I gazed at the charred remains of the senior high-rise, where 125 elderly residents had narrowly escaped a blaze begun from one careless cigarette. I approached respectfully, stunned by the mournful situation, but resisted the temptation to linger or gawk at the tragedies. Suddenly a woman appeared beside me by the security fence surrounding the building. She looked worn, broken, and alone. As she clutched the chain-link fence, she shared her story about the traumatic exodus from the burning building. She needed to tell someone and had chosen me. She had lost everything in the fire; not a single trace remained. Drawn to her misfortune, I felt a nudge to do something to alleviate her suffering. *How could I help her? How could I turn away?*

As a member of the Society of St. Vincent de Paul, a Catholic lay organization serving the poor, I had walked the halls of this building to deliver bags of food and to help with small rent or utility bills. The urgency of the fire was different. Seeing confusion, desperation, and sorrow in the survivors as they dealt with the reality of loss struck me deeply. They needed a comforting presence at that moment. I could be living proof that God had not forgotten them and that someone cared.

Finishing her story, the woman drifted off and went her own way.

After I left that day, a feeling of heaviness followed me, and it would not let go. I felt so unsettled that I had to take it to prayer. I thought about the patron saint of all charitable works, St. Vincent de Paul, who lived four centuries ago yet still felt alive.

Was Vincent listening and how could he help? I admired Vincent's dedication to serving the poor and compassion for others.

The woman at the fence drew me into this tragedy. How could I walk away now? I wanted to hear God's voice. I needed answers.

I attended the first community meeting with the seniors to see how they were coping with the situation and if any plans were underway. This older generation looked so weak and vulnerable with their wheelchairs and walkers that I felt compelled to help. It was a sad reminder of my mother's life of suffering and her death less than a year ago. Although I didn't recognize anyone in the room, I resolved to make a few new friends. The results of a smoldering cigarette had cast a grim shadow over their lives, and if ever they needed help, it was now.

I sensed that God had brought me here for a particular purpose, but this was far beyond my comfort zone. *How was I to address the material or emotional needs of all these people?* I prayed for St. Vincent's divine inspiration. He was a faithful follower of the Gospel who believed that being a saint was easy if one carried out God's will in all circumstances.

So, I needed Vincent's wisdom to discern God's will, to implement it, and to trust in Divine Providence for the necessary provisions.

The work of Vincent de Paul was truly remarkable for his day and age. Despite the numerous demands placed upon him, he transformed the religious life of the Catholic Church in the 1600s and its ministry to the poor. With his humble peasant background and a simple, disciplined nature, he served God and his neighbor with all his heart.

Vincent met Francis de Sales, the bishop of Geneva, in Paris around 1618. Francis was widely known for his *Introduction to the Devout Life,* which Vincent greatly esteemed. The admiration was mutual and the two were kindred spirits. After Francis's death, Vincent gladly testified in his beatification process. "[Vincent] had already met many prelates cloaked in their dignity or learned theologians barricaded behind their science, but here for the first time he was face-to-face with the very image of what he called the Son of God on earth. He would be marked forever by the virtue of Francis de Sales, his mild nature, his goodness, and his humble demeanor, and strive with all his might to conform to this model."[1]

Vincent's encounter with a dying peasant in 1617 was the turning point in his life. Although Vincent had initially sought the priesthood to secure a comfortable lifestyle for himself and to support his poor parents, he had a change of heart after hearing the confession of a dying peasant. Profoundly affected by this encounter, Vincent reflected on what would have happened to this man if he hadn't been there. Afterward, he left Paris and took a position in a poor rural church, where he discovered his true calling: to serve the poor. Vincent's vision of the poor had changed. He began to regard them as his own and could see the face of Christ in them. For Vincent, nothing was closer to the will of God.

Vincent saw the poor as his lords and masters, as Jesus had demonstrated in washing his disciple's feet (John 13:1–17). He reasoned that since Jesus chose to be born poor and had made himself a servant of the poor, every deed that helped or harmed the poor was done for or against Jesus. Vincent is called the Apostle of Charity as he is one of the most influential proponents of charity in history.

"Vincent had the reputation of doing wonders wherever he went, and in his wake he brought together people of goodwill, drawn into action by his example, working to comfort the miserable who suffered in body

---

1   Bernard Pujo, *Vincent de Paul, The Trailblazer.* Translated by Gertrud Graubart Champe (Notre Dame, IN:University of Notre Dame Press, 2003), 76.

and soul."[2] His tireless efforts for those in need also included orphans and galley slaves.

When he was appointed the general chaplain for galley slaves in 1619, he drew on his own experience. He knew the heart of a slave, as fourteen years earlier, Vincent had been captured at sea by Turkish pirates and sold into slavery in northern Africa. He later escaped with his master whom he converted. Those memories left an indelible mark. Vincent worked to improve the living conditions of the slaves, who were subsisting in damp dungeons on dark bread and water. On one occasion, Vincent put on a slave's leg irons to express his unity. Vincent's compassion aroused the consciousness of those around him, as he bent toward patterning his model Jesus Christ.

Vincent had a gift for words and an innate ability to draw the sympathy and understanding of others. He observed that there was not a lack of charity, but a lack of organization. He was a master organizer and a prudent planner; solutions to problems were quickly found. Through bold initiatives, he established and directed a network of charitable foundations. He laid out the road, inviting others to continue the charitable works that he had begun.

Likewise, I share an affinity for organizing and implementing collaborative plans, which would prove essential to aiding senior fire victims.

Vincent knew how to make the proper connections among people and yield fruitful results. Vincent provided spiritual direction for the Ladies of Charity, a pious group of wealthy donors who funded his projects. In 1633, one of the Ladies of Charity, Louise de Marillac and Vincent co-founded the Daughters of Charity, an early non-cloistered order. Their motto "The love of Christ crucified urges us" comes from 2 Corinthians 5:14. Louise recruited and trained uneducated farm girls to

---

2   Bernard Pujo, *Vincent de Paul, The Trailblazer.* Translated by Gertrud Graubart Champe (Notre Dame, IN:University of Notre Dame Press, 2003), 105.

handle the more strenuous tasks of serving the poor. Following Vincent's criteria, she sought "strong, healthy girls, disposed to works of charity, of irreproachable life, and resolved to be humble, to work at cultivating virtue and to serve the poor for the love of God."[3]

St. Catherine Labouré, a Daughter of Charity, introduced the Miraculous Medal to Paris in 1832 after the Virgin Mary appeared to her three times and gave her this mission. In 1833, Blessed Frederic Ozanam founded the Society of St. Vincent de Paul in Paris with his mentor Blessed Rosalie Rendu, another Daughter of Charity. The Miraculous Medal was already at work!

Vincent recognized the potential of combining feminine and masculine gifts throughout his ministry, as seen in the foundational partnership between Vincent and Louise de Marillac and Frederic with Rosalie Rendu. Vincent's brand of service was a balance of gentleness and strength; of nurturing and guidance. Engaging women to address the temporal and spiritual needs of the poor was radical for his time. Such affairs were typically reserved for priests. Knowing that many priests lacked a proper formation, Vincent established the Congregation of the Mission in 1625, to conform their hearts to God and evangelize the poor throughout the countryside.

Vincent died on September 27, 1660, at age eighty (although his birth date has been disputed). Canonization efforts began in 1713 and his body was exhumed from the grave in a perfectly preserved state. He was declared a saint on June 16, 1737. In 1885, Pope Leo XIII named him the patron saint of all charitable works.

St. Vincent left a legacy rooted in charity and social justice, emphasizing the importance of systemic change and consistent with the Gospel and teachings of the Catholic Church. "The Church's love for the poor...is a part of her constant tradition. This love is inspired by the Gospel of the

---

3   Bernard Pujo, *Vincent de Paul, The Trailblazer.* Translated by Gertrud Graubart Champe (Notre Dame, IN:University of Notre Dame Press, 2003), 122.

Beatitudes (Matthew 5:1–12), of the poverty of Jesus, and of his concern for the poor" (*CCC* 2444). Called by the Gospel to serve the poor, St. Vincent encourages others to follow in his footsteps.

In today's post-COVID society, the need to comfort and serve others is more pressing than ever. The world is plagued with loneliness and despair and is challenged by a growing dependence on technology. Social media is rapidly replacing more meaningful forms of communication. St. Vincent's life exemplifies the importance of being present to others with an open heart, especially to those who are different.

As the senior relief effort gained momentum, I discovered a hidden role for myself by which I could contribute to its success. In answer to prayer, I was part of the task force to address needs and find solutions. Losses from the fire, including a prosthetic leg and hearing aids, streamed in. As seniors transitioned to new housing, a pressing need for household items mounted. Everything from beds and sofas to lamps and cookware was in critical demand and referred to as the "unmet needs". Meeting the individual needs of each household would prove challenging.

Inspired by St. Vincent, I became a master at fulfilling unmet needs and finding answers to desperate prayers. A partnership with a major discount furniture retailer emerged. A charity donated a truckload of brand-new household items. Gift cards and monetary donations poured in. A discount mattress company delivered new beds to seniors on their move-in date. My cup overflowed with gratitude as I gathered, stored, and delivered.

God called me to this particular task and St. Vincent was my intercessor. In the eyes of the world, it seemed foolish to work unlimited hours for months without pay. And yet, a blessing would unfold with each new challenge and a resulting leap of faith. Like St. Vincent, I rejoiced in seeing the face of Jesus during senior home visits. Their courage, resilience, and hope were inspiring. This was another link in Vincent's ever-growing chain of love.

I remember them when I say this Vincentian prayer:

Lord Jesus, deepen our Vincentian spirit of friendship during this meeting. Make us responsive to the Christian calling to seek and find the forgotten, the suffering, or the deprived so that we may bring them your love. Help us to be generous with our time, our possessions, and ourselves in this mission of charity. Perfect in us your love and teach us to share more fully in the Eucharistic Sacrifice offered for all.

From the Opening Prayer of the Society of St. Vincent de Paul

Most Sacred Heart of Jesus	*Have mercy on us.*
Immaculate Heart of Mary	*Pray for us.*
St. Vincent de Paul	*Pray for us.*
St. Louise de Marillac	*Pray for us.*
Blessed Frederic Ozanam	*Pray for us.*
Blessed Rosalie Rendu	*Pray for us.*

Charlene Unterkofler's writings reflect the spirit of serving others, especially the poor. As a long standing member and formator for the Society of St. Vincent de Paul, she draws others closer to God through acts of charity. She enjoys being part of the PraiseWriters Catholic Community. Discover more at *gentleservant. com*.

XVI

Journey of Miracles

How St. Charbel Led Us Closer to the Heart of the Father

Heather Lebano

I sat across the small room, feeling the walls close in on me as I listened to the surgeon who had just come from my husband's operating room. His severe but gentle gaze spoke volumes.

He told me, "We were able to get all of the tumor, but it's likely we're looking at an aggressive, recurring brain cancer."

The words hung heavy in the air.

My mind was reeling.

The surgery had lasted more than six hours; the waiting and recovery felt like an eternity. I just wanted to see Jon, even more so after hearing this prognosis, and to be with him when *he* heard the news. I needed to be near him, to hear his voice and know he had made it through.

My mind drifted back to earlier that week, to the moment when a relic—a stone from the tomb of St. Charbel—was touched to Jon's head before we arrived at the ER, before brain cancer entered our lives.

I had only recently learned about St. Charbel through some friends who knew of his intercession in times of illness.

As I sat there processing the surgeon's words, I thought back on those prayers in my family room a few days earlier.

This saint was making himself known to us.

I realized the doctor was still standing in front of me, waiting for me to say something in response to his earth-shattering news.

With a sense of total peace, I looked up at the doctor. I said, "You know, doc, I believe in miracles." The words left my mouth and filled the room as if the Holy Spirit uttered them for me. The doctor looked at me, uncertain how to respond, his eyes briefly meeting mine before he nodded, acknowledging what I had said but unable to respond. I had no idea if he agreed. He didn't need to. He extended his hand in a distant gesture of comfort after questions were answered

The space seemed to close in on me as he left the room. I took a deep breath, closed my eyes, and gathered myself before returning to the waiting room, quietly repeating, "I believe in miracles."

I have always believed in miracles—big and small ones. I counted the ones we had already received: it was a miracle I made it through that moment, we made it through that week, and Jon made it through the surgery. That entire week had been a whirlwind of uncertainties, prayers, and intercession. Jon's emergency surgery, the prayers with the relic, and now this bleak diagnosis.

Despite everything, I believed.

I believed in miracles and the power of prayer.

Sitting in the waiting room, I whispered, "Lord, thank you for getting Jon through the surgery. Thank you for this miracle. St. Charbel, please intercede."

When I finally saw Jon later that night, I was overcome with emotion, trying to wrap my mind around all we had been through that week. He looked remarkably well for someone who had just undergone brain surgery. We finally talked about the news we were handed, and despite the devastating diagnosis, we thanked God for the miracle of him surviving the surgery.

But that following day, the day after the surgery, I found myself searching for hope.

I started thinking of how we were praying with friends less than a week ago with the stone from St. Charbel's tomb held to Jon's head.

Then I remembered it was St. Charbel's feast day.

I remembered he was the patron saint of miracles.

This was a grace.

It was hope.

A supernatural peace washed over me.

Receiving the gift of the saint's stone and having the surgery on his feast day was providential—another gift from God, brought about through the intercession of a saint known for many miracles.

Days before we knew the gravity of what took us to the ER, I stumbled upon a quote from St Charbel that resonated deeply: *"Your journey in this world is the trip of your sanctity."*

As those words turned over in my mind, I knew they were meant for me, for us. Jon's journey with brain cancer would indeed become a journey of sanctification, not just for him but for me as well.

I continue to cling to those words as I navigate this new life of loss as a widow.

St. Charbel, the patron saint of miracles and of Lebanon, was devoted to the Eucharist and fully embraced the cross. Tradition says he carried a cross in his left hand and proclaimed—"take up your cross and follow me" (Matthew 16:24)—with a candle in his right hand to symbolize Christ being "the light of the world."

The image of carrying a cross like Christ and St. Charbel stuck in my head throughout Jon's illness. Jon and I each carried our own heavy crosses; we hoped that our choice to surrender to our cross—united with Christ—could become a light to others, a beacon of hope in our difficult journey.

The night of the surgery, as I lay my head on the pillow, I had asked the Holy Spirit, the Great Comforter, to stay close while pleading to St. Charbel for his intercession. *Remember, I believe in miracles.* That night, I probably prayed more than slept as I processed this journey we were being asked to walk.

As I prayed, I considered how St. Charbel chose a life as a monk and hermit, dedicated to prayer, penance, and the Eucharist, which inspired me. He had lived in total abandonment to God's will, accepting his cross, and I prayed for God to give me the grace to do the same as I walked with Jon through each unknown.

What a perfect intercessor who indeed found us.

As God would have it, while driving back to the hospital the morning after the surgery, I realized I had been passing a small tucked-away Lebanese church named for St. Charbel.

Jon was discharged just one day after St. Charbel's feast, only two days post-surgery, and we were amazed at how well he was doing. Jon asked if we could stop at the church on our drive home. Though the church doors were locked, we parked by the statue of St. Charbel, sat in the car to pray and thank Jesus for getting us through the surgery and for another day.

We both sat quietly, praying and weeping at the magnitude of this cross we were now asked to carry. We begged for mercy, strength, courage, and a huge miracle, if it was God's will. We had never felt closer to God.

As we were leaving to go home, I noticed a plaque near the statue of St. Charbel stating that he was ordained a priest the day before his feast day, the same day as Jon's surgery, a very significant day in St. Charbel's life that had now become a significant day in ours. This was no coincidence—God is in the details.

I made a point of taking that route every day for the next three years of Jon's illness, and each time I passed it, I was reminded of St. Charbel's miraculous intercession.

St. Charbel, Youssef Antoun Makhlouf, was born May 8, 1828, in the small Lebanese village of Bekaa Kafra. From a young age, he felt a strong call to a life of prayer and solitude. At twenty-three, he left home to join the Monastery of St. Maron in Annaya, where he chose the name of a second century martyr, Charbel, whose name means "story (or breath) of God." Joining the monastery was the beginning of a life wholly dedicated to God. St. Charbel's devotion inspired many people, including me and Jon, as he became a great intercessor.

As a Maronite priest, Charbel lived a life of deep humility and devotion to the Eucharist and the Blessed Mother. After sixteen years in the monastery, he sought permission to live as a hermit, and he spent the remaining twenty-three years in a small hermitage dedicating himself to prayer, fasting, and penance. The Eucharist was the center of his life, so he spent hours in Adoration, even during the harshest conditions.

St. Charbel's life was marked by severe mortification and total abandonment to God's will. He fully embraced his cross, carrying it with love and humility. While alone in the hermitage, he kept his companions—Christ in the Eucharist and the Blessed Mother—close.

On December 16, 1898, while reciting the prayer of the Holy Liturgy, St. Charbel suffered a stroke. He died on Christmas Eve, after spending several days in agony, fully accepting his suffering as a way to unite himself with Christ.

Jon too would unite himself to Jesus in his suffering and long illness. After years of battling cancer and embracing his cross, he passed away peacefully surrounded by his family and covered in prayer. I believe that St. Charbel (along with our other saints friends) was present all along, but especially in those final, agonizing but grace-filled moments.

St. Charbel's miracles began shortly after his death. His tomb emitted a bright light for forty-five nights. When his body was exhumed, he was found to be incorrupt, exuding an oily substance that continues to this day. Known as the Miracle Monk of Lebanon, thousands of miracles have been attributed to his intercession, including healings from terminal illnesses, conversions, and spiritual issues. Pilgrims flock to his tomb from all over the world, seeking his intercession and his gift of healing.

Pope Paul VI beatified St. Charbel on December 5, 1965, at the closing of the Second Vatican Council. He described St. Charbel as "a new, eminent member of monastic sanctity, enriching the entire Christian people by his example and his intercession."[1] He is a saint who reminds the world of the value of poverty, penance, and asceticism in a time when riches and comfort often took precedence. St. Charbel's life is a powerful reminder of the essential role of prayer, hidden virtues, and penance in the Christian life.

Looking back on our journey as Jon lived with brain cancer, I see how prayer and intercession were an integral part of our pilgrimage and how it became a path to sanctification for both of us. We both drew closer to the heart of the Father as Jon lived with cancer. God's presence, grace, and miraculous peace were undeniably woven through our lives as we carried that cross together, held by the prayers of others, the intercession of St. Charbel, and most of all, the grace of our Lord and Savior.

St. Charbel's life of deep devotion, humility, love, and light inspires me even as I continue this walk of faith through loss. Jon and I bore the cross of brain cancer, facing another surgery and even a stroke, until he entered eternal life.

This powerful saint reminds us, "Your voyage in this world is a path to holiness, which is a perpetual transformation of the material state toward the state of light."[2] Jon's journey, though filled with suffering, was a journey toward the radiant light of Christ. I continue to walk that path, carrying the lessons and grace we received.

Jon's battle with brain cancer was a long and painful journey, and it was also a journey of grace, mercy, light, and miracles and was his path to holiness and eternity. Through the intercession of St. Charbel and the grace of God, we experienced moments of profound peace and healing, even while suffering. I am reminded of this as I accept my cross now, living without Jon on this side of heaven.

---

1 Catholic News Agency, "St. Charbel Makhlouf," *Catholic News Agency*, accessed October 16, 2024, *https://www.catholicnewsagency.com/saint/st-charbel-makhlouf-534*.

2 *Love is a Radiant Light: The Life and Words of St. Charbel* (Boston: Pauline Books & Media, 2019), 52.

I am grateful St. Charbel was so providentially brought into our lives and lit our path as we faced the unimaginable. To have a powerful saint like him interceding for us was a miracle all on its own.

St. Charbel **is** *the patron saint of miracles.*

Though Jon didn't receive the miracle of complete earthly healing, he *was* made holy and whole. I can look back and see my own healing as my heart was moved by faith and trusting God's will even in the difficult journey. I see how the example and intercession of this saint continue to draw me closer to Jesus on my path toward eternity—my journey of sanctification.

When we pray for miracles, sometimes we get one even greater than we asked for. We want healings and material providence—and sometimes, that's what we get. But sometimes, even when a saint intercedes, God gives or allows not what we want, but what we need—which is Him. We need a life well lived and a holy death. Jon had both.

St. Charbel continues to be a heavenly friend in this great cloud of witnesses, a light for me on my own path to heaven, interceding and reminding me of the big and small miracles that help us each day.

A Prayer for You

May the intercession of St. Charbel, the love of our faithful witnesses, and the grace of God sustain you in every trial.

May you find the courage to carry your cross with full surrender and obedience to God's will, for the cloud of witnesses are in your midst.

May St. Charbel's radiant light guide you to the miracle of grace each day, and to God's supernatural peace and strength on your journey of sanctification.

Heather Lebano shares stories and reflections on faith, family, grief, and healing, offering hope to those navigating life's journey. As a homeschooling mom, writer, and creator of House of Love and Laughter Shop, she inspires others to find beauty and grace even in the unexpected. Through her blog, podcast with her daughter, and handmade goods, she shares the joy of a life rooted in faith and resilience. Discover more and explore her reflections at *houseofloveandlaughter.com*.

XVII

For the Greater Glory of God

How St. Ignatius Taught Me to Pursue a
Military Career for the Right Reasons

Christina Semmens

My journey with St. Ignatius of Loyola began almost forty years
ago when I attended Marquette University, a Jesuit-run liberal
arts institution in Milwaukee, Wisconsin. Being the daughter of parents
who highly valued education, I jumped at the opportunity to receive this
type of education afforded by my receipt of a four-year Army ROTC
scholarship.

I embraced the intellectual rigor of the liberal arts curriculum, and to
my surprise, I relished the challenges associated with my ROTC training.
I particularly enjoyed discovering my aptitude for leading others, and
looked forward to being commissioned as an officer at my graduation.
Classes and ROTC probably would have been the entirety of my college
experience but for one small "blip" that occurred Good Friday of my
freshman year—a profound encounter with Christ that led to being
baptized and received into the Catholic Church on Easter Vigil of my
junior year.

That momentous event occurred two months before I participated in my ROTC Advanced Camp and Cadet Troop Leadership Training. However, despite excelling at both, I discovered by the time I returned to campus in the fall that I was facing a serious dilemma.

That dilemma was whether I would be able to accept a commission and serve in the army if I was going to truly live as a disciple of Christ.

And then St. Ignatius profoundly interceded in my life.

Looking back, I can see that he ensured that I not only had a Jesuit priest to lead me through my discernment, but also that I would be introduced to the discernment practices that are part of the Spiritual Exercises of St. Ignatius of Loyola.

Íñigo López de Oñaz y Loyola was born October 23, 1491, and set about all the usual pursuits for a young man of his times. Íñigo enjoyed dancing, fencing, gambling, the pursuit of young ladies, dueling and involvement in military exercises as he served as a page and then later a soldier. Driven by a desire for fame, along with his leadership qualities and diplomatic skills, he received an appointment as an officer and was given charge of the defense of the town of Pamplona.

Íñigo, now thirty years old, was well on his way to becoming a man of influence in the world—with power, prestige, and position. However, his leg was shattered soon after by a cannonball during a siege of the town, and he then returned to his childhood home of Loyola to recuperate.

During this period of recuperation, Íñigo experienced a profound conversion of heart, mind, and soul that changed his life. He no longer wanted worldly prestige, power, and possessions, but rather desired only to become an exemplary disciple of Christ.

This desire to serve Christ prompted him to go on pilgrimage to the Abbey of Montserrat more than four hundred miles away. Once there, he set aside his worldly possessions before Our Lady of Montserrat, and then went to live as a pauper in a cave in nearby Manresa.

In Manresa, Íñigo practiced extreme forms of mortification and fasting, (practices which severely injured his health and caused him to suffer stomach issues until his death), but he also was graced with the spiritual insights that became the Spiritual Exercises.

The Exercises are a compilation of meditations, prayers, and contemplative practices designed to help people deepen their relationship with God and their commitment to be a disciple of Christ. During the process, an individual is encouraged to encounter God's personal, intimate, and redemptive love, and to respond to that love through a series of choices made during times of intense prayer and silence.

After his spiritual growth from the Exercises, Íñigo realized he needed more formal education, so at the age of thirty-three, he returned to grammar school to learn Latin, followed by a year at the University of Alcalá, and then moved to France to study theology at the University of Paris in 1528.

Two significant events occurred there. First, when he went to France, Íñigo Lopez became known as Ignatius de Loyola. Second, six of Ignatius's friends at the university accepted his invitation to undertake the Spiritual Exercises themselves. The result was men on fire for Jesus who desired to evangelize the world.

They formalized this desire on August 15, 1534, by taking solemn vows to continue this work together. These men became the core of the Society of Jesus—the Jesuits, a society approved by Pope Paul III in 1540. Ignatius was selected as the first Superior General, a role in which he served until his death in 1556.

The cornerstone sentiment of the Jesuits' religious philosophy, *"Ad Maiorem Dei Gloriam"* (AMDG), "for the greater glory of God," has served as a guiding principle for the Jesuit order throughout the centuries, and directly flows from the spiritual choices presented during Spiritual Exercises.

The choices of conversion from personal sin, freely embracing discipleship, rejecting the way of evil—specifically, greed, honors, and pride; deciding to live a life of service with and for Christ; and most significantly, incorporating a self-emptying spiritual poverty rooted in humility; are all made for God's glory and for the salvation of humanity.

Making these choices necessitates using the Exercises' fundamental principles of discernment—awareness, understanding and taking action. Not only can these steps help one properly discern during the Exercises, but they are also applicable for any type of discernment.

These principles, which I was introduced to during my senior year of college, have subsequently shaped my life ever since.

I was given a process through which I could continually grow in my awareness of myself and God's movement in both my interior and exterior life.

These principles have given me the ability to grow in the understanding of my own strengths and limitations; to seek more knowledge about God and His plan for me; and to freely choose the path that will help me become the saint God created me to be.

As a result, I have learned how to take action and how to learn from the results and experiences so that I can pursue holiness each and every day of my life.

I have been blessed to have participated in the Spiritual Exercises in a myriad of ways during the last four decades. This is because through the inspiration of the Holy Spirit and the creativity of many subsequent Jesuits, Ignatius's original thirty-day version of the Spiritual Exercises has been modified to be available in shortened three-day, five-day, and eight-day retreat versions. Most significant has been the development in the last century of a forty-week version of the Exercises that can be undertaken in the midst of ordinary life.

My first experience of this forty-week version of the Exercises in 2000–2001 resulted in my pursuing and receiving a master's degree in theology. My second experience prompted a journey that led me to the work I do today as a Catholic author, spiritual mentor, podcast host, and coach for parish ministry leaders.

So, how did my dilemma about receiving a commission in the army as a disciple of Christ get resolved?

By applying the same principles St. Ignatius learned in Manresa from his own life experience, and then subsequently taught his friends in Paris as they undertook the Spiritual Exercises—which have continued to be taught to others to this day.

The first principle is the need to be aware of both the exterior and interior life, and to acknowledge what response our mind, heart, and soul is having as we simultaneously spend time in the silence of God's presence.

The second principle is to seek understanding of those responses. We strive to do this through discerning what responses are of God and what are not.

The third principle is making a response, or taking action which instructs us to not remain straddled forever between choices, but rather, once we have become aware of our responses and have an understanding of those same responses, we then must take an action. This action(s) then assists in the confirmation of whether we have discerned correctly—in that moment.

The greatest lesson of Ignatian discernment is understanding no discernment is ever final and absolute. Life shifts and adjusts, and we change in the process. So what was once the "right" answer may no longer suit our current life circumstances.

In today's world, many would take that as an excuse to be able to break both short and long-term commitments, but Ignatius is adamant that we are not to be "changing horses midstream." In other words, it is virtually impossible to undergo proper discernment if we are in the middle of a crisis or difficulty. Instead, we should be in a place of stability that allows us the space to discern properly.

I was in that proper place of stability during my senior year of college. As I explored whether I could serve as a military officer and simultaneously be a faithful Christian disciple, I meditated particularly upon Christ's words in Matthew 5:9, "Blessed are the peacemakers, for they shall be called sons of God," and in Paul's letter to the Romans 12:18, "If possible, so far as it depends on you, live peaceably with all."

As I was striving to grow in my awareness, I also sought understanding. First, by seeking out the advice of others—particularly my Jesuit spiritual director and the professor of military science for my Army ROTC unit. I also sought understanding of what it is to be a soldier for Christ and for the army, so I immersed myself in the tenets of just war theory and the ideas of deterrence.

Finally, throughout the year, I continued to take action by moving forward with what was necessary to be done if I was to receive my commission at graduation. I fulfilled course requirements and submitted paperwork expressing my desire for potential assignments post-commissioning, and continued my training.

Through the combination of all these, I discerned that my responses were not of God. Through the awarding of my Army ROTC scholarship before college, my aptitude for my training, and the enjoyment and satisfaction that I found as a leader, and the model and instruction of those who had come before me, it was clear that this was the path forward that God desired for me.

The change, however, that God was prompting me towards through my conversion was for me to embark upon my military career, but not do so for myself; rather, to seek to do it for *Him*.

In other words, rather than striving to pursue honors and prestige for myself alone, I had to be a *humble* servant of Christ and accept my commission so I could care for others as Christ would.

Here again, Ignatius has been my guide. Humility was the hallmark of Ignatius's life.

As he grew in his capacity for discipleship, he also descended deeper and deeper into the self-emptying humility—the key for his own sanctification—and our own.

To become a saint is the ultimate end of discipleship.

Ignatius modeled humility for each of us in his own life. Through the Spiritual Exercises, he has helped to cultivate humility in the souls of countless others across the centuries, including myself, as we seek to follow the footsteps of Christ on the path of humility, while we strive towards holiness.

To help keep me focused upon my need for humility on my journey towards holiness, I offer the Suscipe prayer of St. Ignatius every morning. I invite you to do the same, and to call upon St. Ignatius's intercession to help you discern your decisions, both big and small, and to grow in sanctity as well.

Take, O Lord, and receive all my liberty, my memory, my understanding, and my entire will.

Whatever I have or hold, You have given me; I restore it all to You and surrender it wholly to be governed by Your will.

Give me only Your love and Your grace, and I am rich enough and ask for nothing more.

St Ignatius of Loyola, pray for us!

Christina Semmens is a Catholic author, speaker, spiritual mentor, ministry leadership coach, and host of the *Say Yes to Holiness* and *The Catholic Leadership Puzzle* podcasts. She lives in Fort Payne, Alabama, where she strives to live out a life of authentic discipleship in the pursuit of holiness while empowering, teaching, and accompanying others to do the same. Find out more at *sayyestoholiness.com*.

XVIII

MY WHOLE SELF

How St. Padre Pio Taught Me to Suffer Well

Marti Garcia

Holy, Holy, Holy Lord God of Hosts. Heaven and earth are filled with your glory. Hosanna in the highest. Blessed is he who comes in the name of the Lord, Hosanna, in the highest.

My heart was beating so fast that it was ready to jump out of my chest. I slowly knelt on a rickety old kneeler. In awe of my surroundings, my eyes lifted up to the altar, where two priests were concelebrating Mass. St. Padre Pio had often said Masses on this majestic altar and showed his great passion for the Eucharist.

The deep feeling of humility overwhelmed me. My thoughts were racing to how many lost souls in the past knelt here just like me. *Oh, Jesus, please help me. It has been almost a year since my husband suddenly passed away. We had moved away from my hometown, where you ignited me with so many spiritual gifts. Now, in my current parish, I feel so lost. I don't know where to begin. Help me as I seek spiritual direction.*

At that moment, I knew I was in the right place—San Giovanni Rotondo, Italy—on a pilgrimage with parishioners from my hometown parish, awakening to many possibilities. After Mass, as the crowd left, I stayed behind. I distanced myself from our tour group. Respect and deep faith surrounded me, and I yearned to learn more about Padre Pio's life.

Padre Pio was born in Pietrelcina near Benevento on May 25, 1887, to Grazio Forgione and Maria Giuseppa De Nunzio. At baptism, he was given the name Francesco (Francis). He was drawn to the Eucharist at a young age and decided to become a priest. He joined the Capuchins in 1903, becoming Padre Pio, and was ordained a priest on August 10, 1910, in the Cathedral of Benevento.

From when he was little, Padre Pio experienced supernatural visitors and visions that he thought were normal. He spent his entire life fighting the devil. Along with sickness and sanctions by the Catholic Church, he also joined with Jesus and His sufferings by having the stigmata. He spent hours upon hours hearing confessions and giving spiritual direction.

Many of his friars overheard him plead in prayer: "Jesus, Mary, have pity, O Jesus. I commend to you this soul; you must convert it, save it ... If men have to be punished, punish me. I am content ... I offer my whole self for his sake."[1]

Sitting in a pew deep in prayer, I quickly jumped up to exit the empty chapel and eyed an old dark wood, self-contained structure in the back. In total shock, I realized it was St. Padre Pio's actual confessional, where countless sins were forgiven. I slowly walked up to the confessional and put my hand on the wood, feeling this was possibly the last place he held confession. I had Holy Spirit bumps from head to toe. My life was about to change.

Padre Pio died on September 23, 1968. Pope John Paul II declared Padre Pio a saint on June 16, 2002, with an overflowing crowd at St. Peter's in Rome. St. Padre Pio is the patron saint of healing, suffering, pain, and miracles. He is also the patron saint of civil defense volunteers.

---

1 Fr. Gabriele Amorth, *Padre Pio: Stories and Memories of My Mentor and Friend* (San Francisco: Ignatius, 2021), 62.

I walked outside, took a deep breath, and felt the space between heaven and earth open up. Drops of rain started to fall, and I barely felt them as I began my long walk down a vast cement hill to the Lower Church of St. Pio Pilgrimage Church, where his body lay in rest.

As I began the descent, it represented to me, in my heart and soul, a pilgrimage. Jesus joined and gently spoke to me, "My dear child, I have someone I want you to meet—Padre Pio. He will be your spiritual director. He will guide you." Trying to hold myself up from the outpouring of grace and my overwhelming sense of humility, I realized my face was wet, not from rain, but tears flowing down my cheeks. In awe of our Lord Jesus Christ, I whispered, "Yes."

I took my next step toward the new 6,000-square-foot church, which led me to the entrance corridor. This descent continued inside, leading to the crypt of St. Padre Pio.

Words cannot describe the first impression of this corridor. This winding hallway was full of gold-inlaid mosaic images depicting the different stages of Christ's life through the life of St. Padre Pio on one side and St. Francis of Assisi on the other.

Each mosaic had a brief description that continued to lead me on this pilgrimage. I absolutely had no idea there was a connection between Padre Pio and St. Francis of Assisi. Padre Pio took on St. Francis of Assisi as his mentor from an early age. Seeing the resemblance of their lives, I began to understand that I, too, had similar sufferings.

St. Francis of Assisi has always been a prayer warrior of mine. My grandmother and grandfather were named Francis and Frances. When I was little, I thought I was related to St. Francis! His love for Christ in the Eucharist and guidance to what really matters helped me in my faith. St. Francis assisted me in finding peace and God's love in everything. St. Francis used to say he wanted his followers to go about the world like strolling minstrels "to inspire the hearts of people and stir them to spiritual joy."

Standing in St. Padre Pio's corridor, I thought back about our first tour stop in Assisi to learn about and experience the essence of St. Francis of Assisi. I recalled thinking, *Leave me right here in this beautiful little town of Assisi, Italy. I won't mind missing the bus.*

In the corridor to St. Padre Pio, I also considered how often we would recite the St. Francis Peace Prayer during my Catholic School days. When recited, Francis's Peace Prayer also resonates with me in St. Padre Pio's way.

> *Lord, make me an instrument of your peace,*
> *Where there is hatred, let me sow love;*
> *Where there is injury, pardon;*
> *Where there is doubt, faith;*
> *Where there is despair, hope;*
> *Where there is darkness, light;*
> *Where there is sadness, joy;*
>
> *O Divine Master, grant that I may not so much seek to be consoled as to console;*
> *To be understood as to understand;*
> *To be loved as to love.*
>
> *For it is in giving that we receive;*
> *It is in pardoning that we are pardoned;*
> *And it is in dying that we are born to eternal life.*

As I walked Assisi's cobblestone streets, I felt St. Francis walking beside me, holding my hand and encouraging me that something good would happen. Little did I know our next stop in San Giovanni Rotondo would elevate my faith in impossible ways.

Patiently praying in a long line to see the remains of Padre Pio, I was ushered past the remains of Padre Pio without being allowed to pause. I didn't want to leave. I dashed into a pew, sat down, and closed my eyes in contemplation of being at confession with my pastor back at my parish, pouring out my deep struggles with people attacking me for no reason, which had become a theme in the confessional. He calmly said, "You are a suffering soul."

The statement truly described my life, but the suffering St. Padre Pio experienced was no comparison. He asked to be joined with Jesus.

Sitting with Padre, I saw that the pieces were falling into place. St. Padre Pio was named Francis at birth. St. Francis became a model for St. Padre Pio, and together, their goal in life was to bring the true presence of God into each of our hearts, including mine.

Jesus's sacrifice goes beyond any measure; Padre Pio followed Jesus into that sacrifice out of pure love for him and the crosses they bore together.

Like me, many Catholics have experienced Padre Pio's compassion, sternness, humility, and guidance. He often prayed that he would wait at the gates of heaven until all his children made it into heaven.

"I consider that the sufferings of this present time are not worth comparing with the glory that is to be revealed to us" (Romans 8:18).

From that pilgrimage, I brought back a new awakening of faith, and an understanding of the suffering soul. As I learned more about St. Padre Pio, I also began to recognize his way of communicating with me—his direct way of expressing concern, his fatherly way of putting me back on track. I leaned on him during my times of suffering.

St. Padre Pio understood me then and understands me now. I have followed him in my deep love for the Eucharist, the true Presence. He awaits me in the pew as I return with Jesus in my heart and soul. I am Jesus's vessel, and I know He loves me.

St. Padre Pio carried the ultimate suffering with his stigmata. If you are struggling now, ask for his intercession. He wants to tell Jesus to fill you with the peace and understanding that only comes from the Lord. St. Padre Pio can help you carry your burdens. As he says,

"Pray, hope, and don't worry. Worry is useless. God is merciful and will hear your prayer."

Especially in times of suffering, we can make a pilgrimage to receive greater healing and hope. It needn't be far—even a local church or shrine works. A pilgrimage, a spiritual journey to a holy destination, allows us to open our hearts and encounter God. It may also be a place of deeper encounter with our friends the saints, as I experienced with Padre Pio, who helped me look closely into my interior life and calling as I continue on my earthly pilgrimage. I invite you to consider planning your next pilgrimage. It could be a shrine, a cathedral, or a location that is important to your faith or beliefs. You could even make your Mass next Sunday a pilgrimage. Be open to the beautiful ways of the Lord, and be ready to pack your bags.

Prayer for the Intercession of Padre Pio

Dear God, You generously blessed Your servant, St. Pio of Pietrelcina, with the gifts of the Spirit. You marked his body with the five wounds of Christ Crucified as a powerful witness to the saving Passion and Death of Your Son. Endowed with the gift of discernment, St. Pio labored endlessly in the confessional for the salvation of souls. With reverence and intense devotion in the celebration of Mass, he invited countless men and women to a greater union with Jesus Christ in the Sacrament of the Holy Eucharist. Through the intercession of St. Pio of Pietrelcina, I confidently beseech You to grant me the grace of (here state your petition).

Glory be to the Father ... (three times). Amen.

Marti Garcia's passions are her love for the Eucharist, retired life, and growing deeper in her Catholic faith. Marti is a sacristan and Eucharistic minister, facilitates small groups, and assists as a First Communion catechist for parents. Being a parent educator and writer for thirty-five years she now dedicates her writing time to her faith. You can find her at *MartiGarcia.org.*

XIX

Broken Motherhood

How Our Lady of Sorrows Helped Me Grieve

Michelle Hamel

"How would you like to honor your daughter?"

It was not the question that I was expecting to answer in the spring of 2022, as I sat in my new therapist's office trying to work through some recent family trauma. Our conversation had turned to a life-changing event that happened more than twenty years earlier. I don't remember exactly how the conversation started. Most likely we were talking about how difficult anniversaries of loss and trauma are. Since I had previous experience with that topic, and the fact that the anniversary of my first daughter's birth and death twenty-four years prior was right around the corner, I found myself sharing some of the painful details of my daughter Therese's short life.

I remember being surprised by the strength and depth of the emotions that bubbled up as I talked about Therese's sixteen-day journey in my arms. Twenty-four years was a long time ago. I had walked the long path of grieving and healing for many years after, learning that white-knuckling through the pain of loss was an inadequate coping mechanism, so I hadn't expected the tears that quietly slid down my cheeks. I had expected to end the hour by moving on and lovingly placing Therese's story back into my memories.

Instead, my therapist asked me: "How would you like to honor your daughter?" That simple question became a starting point for a whole new journey. Although we usually placed flowers on Therese's grave around her birthday, I suddenly knew deep inside of me that God was asking for more: the desire to write Therese's story began to grow in my heart again.

As a young mom with three young sons, finding out I was having a baby girl brought much excitement. I loved all the anticipation of the pink outfits, hair bows, and all things frilly! But God's plan for the little life growing inside of me was very different from my own. Our daughter, Therese, was born with a fatal genetic disorder. Her death was a journey of much pain and grief that has marked my life as a mom in many ways. Thankfully, within that time of mourning and suffering, Jesus gave me the grace to come to know His Mother under the title of Our Lady of Sorrows.

Our Lady of Sorrows touched me in such a very profound way after Therese's death. As I read about each of Mary's Seven Sorrows, I felt a deep connection to Mary that I had never felt before. I was able to connect the emotions that I felt through moments of Therese's short life to each one of Mary's Sorrows. That connection made me feel understood in the broken places of my heart. It made me feel less alone in the deep grief I was buried by and helped me through the long suffering that I lived with on the slow path of healing.

After Therese's death, writing her story was really important to me. Her life, while incredibly short, was incredibly meaningful, and I didn't want her to be forgotten. I wanted to share the tangible graces that touched our family and friends who journeyed with us during Therese's time on earth.

Once I had written Therese's story through the eyes of Mary's Sorrows, I had no idea what to do with it. I was a busy, grieving mom who continued to have more babies in the years that followed. So for many years, the words I had written were not shared and Therese's story remained dormant in my heart.

But after pondering my therapist's question, the story of Therese's life weaved within the Seven Sorrows of Mary awoke in my heart. Slowly over the following year, God began opening doors that eventually led to a book deal with Pauline Press and Media.

When God inspired me to write Therese's story in 2022, I was in a deep state of brokenness and in the midst of trying to manage a traumatic situation with our eldest living daughter. God wasn't waiting for me to be healed from my current hurts and grief before He opened a door that He was inviting me to walk through. In fact, He was asking me to return to the second most painful time in my life and start writing about every single detail of those memories in the past while still navigating the grief in my present.

As I wrote Therese's story, God reconnected me with Our Lady of Sorrows. Up until that moment, I thought that my connection to Our Lady of Sorrows was a grace for the time surrounding Therese's loss. Yet, Mary's help and presence in my life all those years ago wasn't just a "one and done" occurrence.

The more time that I spent writing about Our Lady of Sorrows, the more Mary opened my eyes to connect my present day grief to her own suffering and loss in ways I had never before considered.

In providing an opportunity to honor Therese's life, Mary helped me to carry the crushing pain I was feeling over my young adult daughter. Mary is concerned about all of our children, but she is also concerned about the pain our own hearts carry as mothers of wounded and broken children.

I see now that Mary reached out to me in the midst of my broken motherhood. She has tethered me to herself while I do the hard work of grieving and healing as I wait for God to show me how He is going to fulfill the promise of Romans 8:28 in the hurt and brokenness of my family's current situation: "And we know that in all things God works for the good of those who love him, who have been called according to his purpose." I wait to see how God is going to redeem and make new what appears to be an incurable wound to my human heart.

As I wait, I try to keep my eyes on my Mother, who was our ultimate example of how to wait in moments of extreme duress and apparent hopelessness. Mary, as Our Lady of Sorrows, showed all of us how to stay beside the ones we love as she walked the path of Calvary beside her Son. Mary showed us how to persevere through our loved ones' most painful moments as she stood at the foot of Jesus's cross giving Him her whole heart. Mary showed us how to grieve and hold firm to God despite our circumstances as she held Jesus's lifeless body in her arms. Although her heart was pierced, Mary was again the ultimate example of unwavering trust and hope for what God can do, because she did not despair even when she lays Jesus in the tomb and walked away not knowing the details of the next step.

The greatest sorrows of my life have come from watching my children suffer. I have had moments in the last few years that have left me clinging to God in an attempt to survive storms that I wasn't sure that I could, or quite honestly at times, even wanted to survive. Supporting and carrying the pain of my suffering child while my own heart is breaking and grieving is incredibly difficult.

In Season 9, Episode 19 of the *Abiding Together* podcast, Sr. Miriam James Heidland spoke of Satan as a sniper. She shared, "The evil one, the enemy, can perceive what our destiny might be and where we're called to bear life and what our future might look like. And it is in this very place where he will sow his deepest lie and fire his most painful bullet ... Your wounds are not arbitrary. They didn't just happen."

When I learned of the trauma that my daughter went through, as a mother, it broke me. I felt it as a direct hit sent by the enemy that shattered my identity as a mother, as well as my heart. But Mary as Our Lady of Sorrows, reached into my brokenness and continues to accompany me on the painful path I find myself on. Her Sorrows give all of us an example to follow as we navigate the grief and loss of any traumatic circumstance we find ourselves living through. Knowing that Mary understands a mother's suffering and grieving heart can be a source of comfort and consolation for all of us.

At this point in my journey, there's one Sorrow that I find myself drawn to the most. In the Sixth Sorrow of Mary, Jesus is taken down from the Cross and laid in Mary's arms. I can imagine the devastating grief and heartache that rips through her entire soul as she holds her lifeless, beloved Son in her arms for the final time. The perfect love of her Son was met with anger, hatred, and unspeakable violence that marked every inch of His body.

Nevertheless, Mary does not rant and rail at all the soldiers or the crowd that jeered Jesus in the last hours of His life. Her focus is always on loving her Son. When I consider the posture of Mary's heart at that moment, I can't help but think that she would imitate her Son. Despite the immense grief and pain that pierced her heart, I can imagine that she whispered the words of her Son, "Father, forgive them; for they know not what they do" (Luke 23:34).

I have found myself imagining holding my own daughter in her pain and brokenness, as I whisper those words of mercy for those that have caused her wounds. Saying those words hasn't in any way invalidated what she has suffered nor what I have suffered as a result of her trauma, but imagining that scene and speaking those words has allowed me to surrender my pain to God and entrust Him to take care of it.

I have been able to begin the shift from an incredibly painful, stagnant internal focus of "why" this devastating trauma happened, to being able to look up and ask God "*how*" He will redeem a situation that seems so impossible. I'm no longer trying to fix and figure out the situation as if it all depended on me. I have surrendered it to God who is the true healer. (And on the frequent occasion that I forget and grab the illusion of control back into my hands, God waits until I surrender it all to Him again and then encourages me in the waiting.) This surrender is a gift from Our Lady of Sorrows.

Our Lady of Sorrows reaches out to us, waits with us, and consoles us in every moment of grief and loss in our lives. And while I do not have the unwavering faith that Mary has, she wants to help all of us as we navigate the brokenness in our lives. She is with us particularly in the crosses we carry as parents, as we watch our children suffer—whether physical suffering and even death, or other kinds of trauma and emotional crucifixions. She knows what it is to bear the unspeakable grief of a parent at the foot of another's cross. She reminds us on our worst days to look up and cling to the hope that God can and will resurrect and redeem our seemingly hopeless situations in His time.

Lord, thank you for the gift of your mother and for her example of faith and fortitude in times of deep grief and loss. Please help us to cling to her when the circumstances of our life cause us deep pain. Please revive us and redeem us from the brokenness we carry that feels so hopeless.

Our Lady of Sorrows, pray for us.

Michelle Hamel is a wife and mother who writes to encourage women in all seasons of life, especially those times of grief and struggle. She is the author of a forthcoming book about the journey of infant loss accompanied by Our Lady of Sorrows. Find Michelle at *michellehamel.com*.

XX

THE FLAME

How St. John of the Cross Sparked a
Love of Prayer and Poetry

Rose Ann Heisel

Sleet assaulted my car as I drove towards a retreat at the neighboring church. The wind pulled my wheels and threatened to spin me off the road. Tightly gripping the steering wheel, I asked Jesus if this was a wise choice. In my heart I heard, "You need to be there; it will be worth the trouble." I just could not imagine what was in store for me that day.

I never expected to be introduced to St. John of the Cross.

The seminar began after Mass. I remember well the last talk of the morning. A priest mentioned an experience of St. Phillip Neri, and as he spoke, I felt the presence of the Holy Spirit deep within my heart. *Could this be part of why God told me I needed to be here?*

St. Philip had a mystical experience in 1544 in the catacombs of the church of St. Sebastian in Rome. As he prayed, a ball of fire descended and entered his mouth, settling in his heart. He was filled with such intense love for God, he fell to the ground. He cried out, "Enough, Lord, I can bear no more!"

As I sat there that stormy afternoon, I remembered another day filled with torrents of rain, long before, when I had particularly felt the burning

145

presence of God's love. I was unfamiliar with the powerful feelings I was experiencing and had never been able to explain it or understand it. I was filled with wonder at the priest's story.

After Father's talk, he headed to the back of the church for lunch. I moved so quickly to catch him that it was almost as if my guardian angel lifted me to my feet and pushed me out of my pew. I met the priest, and I shared with him how his story had illuminated some of my own experiences. Father spun around on his heels, ran back to the front pew, and returned with a well-worn book by St. John of the Cross called *The Living Flame of Love*.

I went home and ordered the book immediately. When it arrived, I read it in one sitting, discovering a deep love for St. John's writing and finding his spirituality fascinating and clarifying. What John taught me was that I had experienced the fire of God's love. Through this Spanish Carmelite mystic, I had truly received a gift from God.

In the year 1542, St. John of the Cross was born on the feast day of St. John the Baptist. He was baptized Juan de Yepes y Alvarez in Spain, very close to the town of Avila, the home of the great St. Teresa of Avila.

Much suffering had taken place in John's early childhood. Early on, he lost his brother Luis and his father, who died after a long illness. The family fell into deep poverty. John, his older brother Francisco, and his mother took care of the family doing whatever work they could find.

John attended an orphanage school for the poor. He received food, shelter, and some training in carpentry and tailoring, but John's gentle, patient way led him to pursue a life of caring for the sick and those in need of spiritual development.

In his teens, John went to live in the Hospital of Conception. As he cared for those suffering from the plague and other diseases, John's compassion was remarkable, and his duties were increased. John always offered encouraging words and a little sense of humor to help brighten the lives of patients. While changing bandages and binding wounds, he was healing their hearts as well. He often took to the streets to beg for money for the hospital in the few spare moments he had.

The hospital wanted John to serve as a chaplain, and as a result, he entered the Carmelites—an order originated by hermits dedicated to Mary and to contemplative life. Eventually, he was ordained by the Carmelites. When he encountered Teresa of Avila, she was looking for someone to lead a reform among the Carmelite friars as well as the nuns, which attracted John who had been drawn to a more ascetical life himself.

Aware of John's deep spirituality, St. Teresa assigned him to be a confessor and a spiritual director to the Convent of the Incarnation in Avila. There, John said Mass, heard confessions, and taught catechism to local children. John helped even Teresa herself to enter into a deeper prayer life.

St. John and two other friars began to restore a house in Duruelo. The house was in poor condition, but John loved the manual labor and delighted in making the grounds a beautiful reflection of God's creation and a wonderful location for deep prayer. As the chaplain, John encouraged the other friars to spend time outdoors.

Sadly, there was jealousy and tension from the unreformed Carmelite Friars. They considered John to be a rebellious man and were watching closely his collaboration with Teresa. Those friars removed John from the grounds and threw him into prison for nine months. He endured whippings and was left hungry in a putrid smelling cell. The only light leaked into the room from a crack in the wall near the ceiling.

In his world of dark emptiness, from the very bowels of his cell, his poetic masterpieces began to take shape.

A changing of the guard brought a new jailer, who showed compassion towards John. He gave him a pen and paper for journaling. One night, John was able to escape. He hid with the Discalced nuns in Toledo who gave him the medical help he needed. After recovering his health, John continued to help Teresa to reform the order and establish new houses.

After a long life of service to God, the Church, and the order he helped to reform, John became ill from a wound on his leg that became infected. His trust in God gave him peace as his health declined and he entered his final days. As he died, he rejoiced with humility that he would get his wish to die after much suffering and in a place where he was unknown. Pressing a cross to his chest, he uttered the words of Jesus: "Into your hands, O Lord, I commend my spirit" (Luke 23:46).

St. John of the Cross left a remarkable legacy. His work reforming the Carmelites made a massive impact on the Church, as did his spiritual writings, but it was his poetry that made the biggest impact on me. John's poetry came from his heart during his time of mediation and prayer in his dank cell. Filled with the Holy Spirit, even in the dark silence, He wrote powerful words, filled with emotion and expressing a deep spiritual maturity. What he taught me was that there is beauty even in darkness, and that I must keep my soul in peace.

In particular, John's incredible poetry, such as the first Stanza from *The Living Flame of Love,* began to speak to me in a very deep way:

> *O Living flame of love*
> *That tenderly wounds my soul in its deepest center!*
> *Since now you are not oppressive,*
> *now consummate! If it be your will:*
> *Tear through the veil of this sweet encounter!*[1]

The more I read St. John of the Cross, the more I too started to feel an overwhelming desire to express my deep encounters with the Lord on paper. I needed to record what I felt burning in my soul. Soon the words came faster than I could write.

Often words flew from my fingers onto the keyboard as I tried to catch up with the stream of words that poured out of my heart in the form

---

1 *The Collected Works of St. John of the Cross.* Translated by Kieran Kavanaugh, O.Carm. and Otilio Rodriguez, O.Carm. (Washington, DC: ICS Publications, 1991), 641.

of poetry. John had unveiled for me a hidden gift and taught me a new way to pray.

Many times now, I use these poems as prayers, as love songs to the Lord. During Lent, my meditations on Jesus in the desert came from deep with my heart:

My footprints are not embedded in your footprints
My walk is shackled to the very stones I fall over
The distance I travel is nonexistent
Why am I blind to your being, your voice?
Are you there?
No where do I see your narrow path
My misery makes me lonely
Come meet me where I am...

Now, I often give poems away to others, hoping they will benefit from the words and stanzas, just as John's words have blessed me.

Out of the storm on that treacherous wintry morning, my prayer life was illuminated through a chance encounter with a mystical poet. No longer was I in darkness about my experiences or without a way to express them. In a way, St. John of the Cross taught me a new language. I encourage readers not to shy away from his poetry, but to explore it as a way to deepen their prayer and give expression to their deepest desires.

Rose Ann Heisel writes her poetry to bring messages of love to the hearts of those who are searching for God in a deeper way. A retreat leader and a published freelance writer, she enjoys photography, time with grandchildren and a small hobby farm with her husband, Steve. She feels abundantly blessed every day by God's glorious creations.

XXI

Conformed to His Heart

How St. John the Beloved Showed Me True Rest

Amanda Villagómez

I closed my eyes, as the narrated scene took shape in my mind. While serving as a chaperone at a high school youth conference, I received Emily Wilson Hussem's invitation to imagine being in a boat with Jesus. I was deeply moved as she invited us to hand over our hearts to the Lord.

I acknowledged all that was pressing on my heart and that I had spent a lot of time and energy playing it out in my mind. As I visually followed her promptings, I recognized that I was willing to hand it all over, but in doing so, I noticed the weight of all those concerns creating a sense of clutter. They seemed like obstacles blocking me from focusing on Jesus and being fully present to him.

Rather than passing them over to Jesus, I perceived a desire to set them aside, leaving only our hands and my heart. I knew the idea was to withdraw my hands, but I did not want to. I wanted to remain connected.

Emily then proceeded to guide us through a moment in which the Lord was rowing the boat, encouraging complete trust in Him. I found myself desiring to recline on His chest, allowing Him to row and just rest on Him, not worrying about where we were going or the route we would take to get there.

Then, I realized I didn't even actually want Him to be rowing at all. Instead, I wanted His hands free to embrace me, letting go of the desire for a certain pace. I was content to have the boat drift in order to more fully receive His love.

Despite that vision, I live much of my life with a full schedule—the natural consequence of being a wife, mom, and teacher educator. I thirst to learn and create. My engagement is easily sparked, but then it all becomes too much to be sustainable. I recognize the need to reel in my passions. Often, it is challenging for me to enter into imaginative prayer, but in that moment, I was receiving clear invitations: Set it aside. Pause. Rest.

All of this resonated as I had just recently begun The Well, an eight-week mentorship program through Blessed is She, facilitated by Beth Davis. The theme that was coming up for me as I prayed through the content was my desire to rest on Jesus's chest like St. John at the Last Supper. Just two days before the prayer exercise at the youth conference, I attended one of the sessions for The Well.

During that meeting, I vulnerably shared how exhausted and burnt out I was feeling. "I have this strong sense that God was really inviting me into rest, but all the multiple pathways I thought He was calling me to and that I was walking towards or trying, all ended up being 'no's. I feel like He does want to give me rest, but I just don't see how, right now," I said.

Beth wisely responded, "I wonder if maybe you're looking for rest in very practical ways, and I do think that's coming. I don't know when, I don't know how, but there is the promise of a deeper interior rest as well, so be open to that too—how the Lord might want to give you rest that way."

Her comment sparked the realization that the rest the Lord most desired to give was not necessarily physical in the way I had envisioned it. My circumstances were not necessarily going to change, but He desired to meet me there and provide me with rest in Him.

Beth had mentioned that she and Emily were friends. I appreciated where Beth left off in an intimate space of a small group of eleven women, Emily picked up, speaking to my heart while simultaneously speaking to more than a thousand others. I pondered in awe the way the Lord uses it all to weave together threads of messages from different contexts to reach our hearts.

Over the years, St. John quietly slipped into my life—perhaps through the way he captured Jesus's life in his Gospel where he documented his relationship with the Lord. Soon after St. John famously leaned on his chest at the Last Supper (John 13:23), Jesus said, "In my Father's house are many rooms; if it were not so, would I have told you that I go to prepare a place for you? And when I go and prepare a place for you, I will come again and will take you to myself, that where I am you may be also" (John 14:2–3). These words have especially taken root in my heart coupled with the chapter immediately after, in which St. John highlighted more of Jesus's message that point towards relationship: "Remain in me, as I remain in you ... Remain in my love" (John 15:4, 9).

I often find myself meditating on the relationship between Jesus and St. John. There is an image of the Last Supper below the tabernacle in my church, capturing the moment in which St. John is reclining on Jesus's chest. Frequently, I intentionally sit in a location where I can ponder that scene during Mass or quiet contemplation before the tabernacle.

Nonetheless, I often find myself in a point of tension between resting with the Lord and action. I have realized that I will perceive a hint of what is to come in prayer but then go racing ahead with how I imagine it is meant to unfold, painfully arriving at the realization that I have sped right into a door that is firmly closed. Often, He meets me in that pain and reminds me that He is answering the deeper prayers. He gives gentle glimpses into the ways in which what I perceived would come to be but in a way and pace different from what I had envisioned.

Jesus once called John and his brother James "sons of thunder." I wonder if St. John struggled with similar tensions as I have—having deep passions that sometimes lead to singular focus and a perceived clear pathway to work towards certain goals before learning this was not quite what Jesus had in mind. The brothers' request to be the ones to sit at Jesus's right and left (Mark 10:35–37) might be an example of this. Yet, along the way, Jesus taught John to be docile. Jesus revealed His heart, and through that intimacy, helped John to receive his identity and mission.

For many years, I focused on what Jesus was *saying* in the Gospel of John. With time, I have come to see the beauty in how those words were captured precisely because of how they took root in St. John's *heart*. There were others who were present for the same scenarios, but St. John was the one who so beautifully captured Jesus's words and actions during the Last Supper. I wonder if St. John's receptivity, the capacity for those words to sink in, were what allowed him to go to the foot of the Cross.

As Jesus walked with him, St. John saw that he could first receive Jesus's love and then receive whatever path was in store for him. Jesus shaped his heart in a way that he was able to recline on His chest, while also being able to go to the foot of the Cross and live suspended in the unknown of what was taking place in the Paschal Mystery but trusting that Jesus would somehow fulfill the promises He had made. The security of his relationship with the Lord allowed him to race towards the tomb upon St. Mary Magdalene's proclamation but then pause and allow St. Peter to enter first (John 20:1–10).

I tend to layer on more and more with each invitation I receive, and I can quickly become tired and overwhelmed. Before too long, I once again received the invitation to move at the pace of intimacy. Yes, Jesus has a plan for my life, but at the center of those plans are the relationship that He wants to develop with me and the ways that He wants to pour out His love in order to sustain me. He wants to co-create with me, while also revealing the mystery that the work He so often wants to do through me is not just a gift for others but also for myself. A gift of love—both giving and receiving, as St. John captured. "Beloved, let us love one another; for love is of God, and he who loves is born of God and knows God" (1 John 4:7).

St. John's life—and the words of Jesus that he captured—continually remind me to trust. Jesus has created a place in the Father's house just for me, and He is leading me there. However my life unfolds, however confusing it may be, I can trust that He is with me, He knows where we are going, and He will help me to arrive. He enters into my unique life and reveals His capacity to love me through the mystery of it all.

The promise is the same for you. We share the invitation to walk with Him and to learn to delight in where He leads us (even when it's hard), just as St. John did.

I invite you to pray this "Litany of Dreams" as you reflect on your story with the Lord and seek to see the beauty in your unique process of becoming that He is leading you on.

Dream with me, Jesus.

That I may be on fire for love of you
Light me up, O Lord.

That my heart may be open to your invitations
Light me up, O Lord.

That I may be in awe at your designs
Light me up, O Lord.

That I may have the courage to go where you lead
Light me up, O Lord.

That I may delight, rather than despair, in your surprises
Light me up, O Lord.

From discouragement
Protect me, O Lord.

From lies that threaten to hold me back
Protect me, O Lord.

From obstacles to your plans
Protect me, O Lord.

From confusions
Protect me, O Lord.

From the tendency to place my identity in my work
Protect me, O Lord.

Through my desires
Purify my heart, O Lord.

Through your timing
Purify my heart, O Lord.

Through what you reveal to me about myself
Purify my heart, O Lord.

Through celebrating the work you are doing in others
Purify my heart, O Lord.

Through perseverance in times of trial and disappointments
Purify my heart, O Lord.

That I may be rooted and grounded in you
Give me the grace, O Lord.

That I may consider it all joy
Give me the grace, O Lord.

That I may view abiding in you as the goal
Give me the grace, O Lord.

That I may trust in you when my heart is broken
Give me the grace, O Lord.

That I may withhold nothing from you
Give me the grace, O Lord.

That I may live with a Thy will be done heart
Let it be done to me, O Lord.

That I may be united to you
Let it be done to me, O Lord.

That I may love you well
Let it be done to me, O Lord.

That my eyes may be fixed on you through this adventure that you are leading me on
Let it be done to me, O Lord.

That you may conform my heart ever more closely to yours all the way to eternity
Let it be done to me, O Lord.

Most Sacred Heart of Jesus, **have mercy on me.**
Most Immaculate heart of Mary, **pray for me.**
Most Chaste Heart of St. Joseph, **pray for me.**
St. John, the Beloved, **pray for me.**
Amen.

Amanda Villagómez writes to celebrate her story with God and to help others connect with theirs. Founder of Endure in Hope and author of *Do the Next Thing: Stepping Forward in Faith*, Amanda loves encouraging people to experience Christ-centered growth and healing through relationship with Him. Find out more and download your copy of the "Litany of Dreams" at *endureinhope.com.*

XXII

WARRIOR OF HUMILITY AND GRACE

How St. Thérèse Taught Me That the Little
Way Is Not for the Faint of Heart

Laurie Ann Pandorf

I pulled into the parking lot of the retreat house, weary from the weekend traffic. Of course, the GPS was correct, but I insisted otherwise and rerouted, adding two more hours to the trip. I had been looking forward to these three days of silence for months and wasn't going to let an orthopedic boot or a PICC line stop me.

Strapping bags across my body, hobbling in on crutches, I soldiered on, up to my room to unpack. Journals, pens, alcohol wipes, saline injections, and bulbs of liquid antibiotics, all present and accounted for, but the surprise attack was waiting.

After I mustered the gumption to return to my car for one more item, I made my way back to the parking lot. *Where did he put it?* Frantically searching the back of the car, blaming my husband, and muttering some "not so nice" words under my breath, it hit me—my bag was MIA. *What! Are you kidding me, God? Haven't I dealt with enough disruption?* Angry and frustrated, I retreated to my room, dropped into the chair, and cried ... utterly defeated.

During dinner, before we entered into the silence, I shared my saga with two young women at the table who graciously listened. In addition to my current crisis, they learned all about my failed foot surgeries, lack of healing, and infections coinciding with my son's mental health decline and intestinal blockages. Mother and son wounded, scarred, and battle fatigued.

In the first gathering that night, our retreat director urged us to "beg for the grace we needed" and to embrace the silence, making space to listen for the whisper of God's voice. It was the first weekend following Easter, reserved for *resurrection joy* and *new life,* two promises I was desperately seeking.

Reeling from the emotions of the day, I sat quietly, waiting for the room to empty before gathering my crutches and bag.

"Laurie," Trish whispered, speaking for Andrea as well, "This is for you." I peeked inside, quietly thanking them for the gift bag. My two new friends had surprised me with a care package complete with toiletries, pajamas, and a sweater for the morning. But inside, tucked away was the real treasure—a prayer card of the Little Flower inscribed with her words of wisdom, *Everything is a Grace.*

Sobbing, I hugged my angels, returned to my room, then struggled to read through that prayer in its entirety, my voice catching at the parts about her "burdens and needs." Despite all the familiarity with my old friend, St. Thérèse of Lisieux, this prayer about humility and grace had eluded and surprised me.

I was first introduced to St. Thérèse in my early twenties when Shirley, a coworker and spiritual mother, shared the novena with me, recopied so many times it was barely legible. I was intrigued by this devout Carmelite's mission to shower roses down from heaven, as noted in the prayer, and to "spend her heaven doing good upon earth."[1] Such a powerful message of hope and promise, especially given her youth and short life.

---

1 John Clarke, *Story of a Soul: The Autobiography of Saint Thérèse of Lisieux* (Washington, DC: ICS Publications, 1996) 263.

Although I was never a *student* of Thérèse, I was mysteriously drawn to her, curious about the parts of her history that interested me. She was my special saint, interceding on my behalf for the mundane as well as the complicated problems that emerged in my life. And here she was again, coming to my rescue, stepping in with spiritual reinforcements.

Having died in 1897, at only twenty-four, her simple, cloistered life was shared with the world when *Story of a Soul*, a series of three manuscripts compiled as an autobiography for her Carmelite community, was formally published one year later, garnering wide attention from religious and laity, catapulting her to an unprecedented early canonization in 1925.

Marie Françoise-Thérèse Martin was the youngest of nine children, with four older sisters and four siblings who predeceased her. Her parents, Louis and Zelie Martin, raised their children in a devout Catholic home. Since both had seriously contemplated vocations before marriage, they were intentional about their faith, attending daily Mass, practicing liturgical rituals and joining pilgrimages. Remarkably, all five daughters entered religious life, four as Carmelites in the same convent, and one as a Visitation Sister.

Story of a Soul recounts Thérèse's life as a child, who struggled with illness, anxiety and loss, as a teenager driven by a relentless desire to enter religious life, as a Carmelite nun carefully honing her "little way" of living, and as a future saint, who bravely suffered and died a painful death from tuberculosis.

At first glance, it is easy to misinterpret her "little way" as an immature kind of faith, or the pronouncement of sending roses as a sweet gesture. After all, her beliefs are firmly rooted in Scripture from Matthew, "For although you have hidden these things from the wise and the understanding, you have revealed them to the childlike" (11:25). However, after examining her writings, letters, and conversations more closely, it becomes clear to many, including two popes, that her simple insights convey a sophisticated understanding of Jesus, discipleship, suffering and spiritual growth—extraordinary gifts from an ordinary life.

As ordinary as she might have appeared, this seemingly gentle introvert possessed the heart of a warrior, emboldened by humility and grace.

After being called to the faith but uncertain in direction, this young defender wrote: "I feel within me, other vocations. I feel the vocation of the warrior, the priest, the Apostle, the doctor, the martyr. I feel within my soul the courage of the crusader, the papal guard, and I would want to die on the field of battle in defense of the Church."[2]

Some of that boldness can be traced to another famous French woman, St. Joan of Arc, who Thérèse idolized. Though not declared a saint during Thérèse's lifetime, the cause for her canonization was active in the public eye. At Carmel, Thérèse honored Joan by writing and performing in two plays and authoring many poems in her defense such as this excerpt from her first draft:

Canticle to Obtain Canonization of Joan of Arc

A heart of fire, a warrior's soul
You gave them to the timid virgin
Sweet Martyr, our monasteries are yours
You know well that virgins are your sisters
And like you the object of their prayers
Is to see God reign in every heart"[3]

Her zeal for the martyrs was highlighted while on a pilgrimage to Rome. Although the family trip was famous for Thérèse seeking the pope's approval to enter Carmel early, there was an incident at the Colosseum that revealed her desire to imitate the brave souls who died for their faith. While on tour, Thérèse and her sister Céline snuck away and climbed down a roped-off area to get to the arena floor, which was

---

2   *Story of a Soul,* 192.
3   Maureen O'Riordan, "St. Therese of Lisieux and St. Joan of Arc-for the feast of St. Joan of Arc," St. Therese of Lisieux: A Gateway, May 30, 2016, http://www.thereseoflisieux.org/my-blog-about-st-therese/2016/5/30/st-therese-of-lisieux-and-st-joan-of-arc-for-the-feast-of-st.html. (accessed October 28, 2024).

under construction. They quickly searched and found the spot, marked by a cross, where the martyrs fought.

Falling to her knees, Thérèse recalled, "My lips touched the dust, stained with the blood of the first Christians. I asked for the grace of being a martyr for Jesus and felt my prayer was answered!"[4] Earlier in that memory, Thérèse compared her desire to be as close as possible to the martyrs to that of Mary Magdalene, who stayed near the tomb of our Lord. Both of them yearned to share in the burden of sacrifice and loss for Jesus.

That confident spirit was apparent even as a toddler, when Thérèse boldly proclaimed, "I choose all," when her sister offered her an item from a basket of doll-making materials. Years later, when Thérèse reflected on that reaction, in response to sacrificing to become a saint, she said, "My God, I choose all! I don't want to be a saint by halves. I'm not afraid to suffer for You, I fear only one thing: to keep my own will; so take it, for 'I choose all' that You will!"[5]

Isn't that the ultimate act of humility—to accept and surrender everything to Jesus—blessings, joys, pain, sorrows, questions, answers... everything?

Thérèse understood that humbling herself was critical for spiritual growth. Her austere life in the monastery was already stripped of worldly possessions, so therefore, interiorly she desired poverty.

Poverty was intentionally practiced in her daily walk, which consisted of tiny sacrifices such as, eating food that others refused, cleaning up messes she didn't create, taking blame for misplaced or broken items in the convent, caring for sisters who were unkind, and remaining in the novitiate, obligated to take direction, long after it was required.

As Thérèse travailed this walk, willingly embracing poverty and humiliation, she naturally grew in grace. Although she can recall with great clarity the moments in her life when God mysteriously intervened

4 *Story of a Soul,* 131.
5 Ibid., 27.

with grace to heal her from mental and physical illnesses, she was also quite aware when grace was bestowed more intimately in response to her "little way" of love and obedience.

Maybe grace, as a foundation for Thérèse's spirituality, can be understood by reflecting on her full Carmelite name: Sister Thérèse of the Child Jesus and of the Holy Face. That title embodies both the child-like faith that Jesus encourages us to embrace as well as a participative faith in joining Him on the road to Calvary. In one instance, we need to fully rely on the Father, surrendering everything, and in another, we need to imitate Jesus by picking up our crosses and sharing in His suffering, a powerful exchange of graces.

Up until that point, I was not fully aware of St. Thérèse's deep spirituality. However, even though I had not fully appreciated the maturity of her "spiritual childhood" until that retreat, I had always called upon her and she had never let me down. As a twenty something, she rescued me from a devastatingly dark depression. She intervened to save our family home and heal my mother of her alcohol addiction.

In my thirties, she was with me when I gave birth to each of my children after complications from C-sections. She assured me that my father-in-law's kidney cancer was contained. She inspired me to write a poem for the unborn, still yet to be shared publicly. And when I finally graduated from college with my first degree at age forty, she was the subject of the keynote address celebrating her as a Doctor of the Church.

Looking back on those moments, it's only now that I'm coming to realize how her insights and spirituality have influenced my growth and knowledge of the faith, especially on suffering, self-reliance, and grace, all of them big topics for someone known for her "little way." Only one with a warrior's heart and courage could intercede to that degree and go to battle for me.

Throughout that retreat, I filled my journal with fifty pages of reflections, many of them tear-stained as I was releasing a great deal of pain, and experienced a deep cleansing that was necessary in order to make room for new wisdom.

I discovered that I had been guilty of keeping God at an arm's length instead of inviting Him in to take the lead. I was also learning to look at my suffering as a means for God to extend his grace, His perfect love for me.

When reflecting on prayer, Thérèse once said, "My strength lies in prayer and sacrifice; they are invincible weapons, and touch hearts more surely than words can do, as I have learned by experience."[6]

Now when I reach out to my dear saint, I think of two distinct images: (1) as a young girl with a sweet smile, confident as a child of God and (2) as a warrior, Joan of Arc, defiantly wielding a sword at her side—two powerful reminders of her way of humility and grace as depicted in the prayer shared with me while on retreat:

Everything is a Grace ...

Everything is the direct effect of our Father's love, difficulties, contradictions, humiliations, all the soul's miseries, her burdens, her needs, Everything, because through them, she learns humility, realizes her weakness. Everything is a grace, because everything is God's gift. Whatever be the character of life or its unexpected events—to the heart that loves, all is well.

The spirituality of St. Thérèse of Lisieux

Laurie Ann Pandorf is continually amazed at discovering the hidden gems of our Catholic faith, including friendship with the saints. After her reversion eleven years ago, she is an active lector, prayer group leader, and retreat team mentor as a writing coach. She recently launched *thewellofgrace.com*, where she hopes to share her daily walk with fellow sojourners.

---

6 *Story of a Soul*, 240–241.

XXIII

LIGHT OF COMPASSION

How St. Clare's Intercession Healed Me

Ruth Ellen Naef

It was 2:45 in the morning.

I awoke and easily sat up, noticing that I felt better than I had in a long time. Then I heard Jesus speak to my heart, "You don't need your walker to go into the bathroom." It was true. I got out of bed on my own and walked—without having to think about each step!

Standing two feet from the sink, I marveled that I wasn't leaning on anything! I stared at myself in the mirror in awe. I was even standing straighter; my balance was better! *How could this be? Is this real?!* I wondered.

Again, I felt God invite me to trust, so I walked the considerable distance to the chapel using my walker, which was far beyond my normal abilities. I thanked, praised, and sang to the Lord!

I cannot fully explain the feelings of wonder and delight that morning, as I was given the strength to kneel on the altar stairs and prostrate myself before the Tabernacle. *Thank you, Jesus ... Why me?*

I knew it was for God's glory, but this healing was also an expression of the Lord's incredible love—the profound love that He has for each of us.

Just the day before, there on the Women of Grace retreat, I had been sitting in my wheelchair, holding the rosary in my hands while praying the Divine Mercy Chaplet. To others it must have appeared I was still praying, my eyes closed as everyone passed me, but in truth I was feeling the extreme exhaustion of my mitochondrial disease. Karen and Kathie, two retreatants, tenderly looked after me. When I was able to speak, I told them I couldn't even move my arms. Tears trickled from my eyes as they comforted me.

Realizing I might miss the upcoming healing service if I didn't get some desperately needed rest, I had gone back to my room. There, Johnnette Benkovic Williams, the founder of Women of Grace, saw my pain and prayed for me. Thea, her daughter, generously asked how she could help. Comforted by their concern, I slept deeply for a couple hours, waking up just before Thea's phone call explaining the healing service would start soon.

At the service, while sitting directly in front of Jesus in the Blessed Sacrament, I heard Fr. Ken saying, "Someone with a neck problem is being healed." Instantly, I knew he meant me! I always suspected my neck was the cause of my fibromyalgia symptoms. Although my neck was still stiff when I went to bed that night, I trusted.

The morning of my healing, as my "sacred sisters" on retreat awakened and we greeted each other, I hugged them, sharing the miracle and wonder of God's love.

At breakfast, the miraculous news spread, announced with joy by Thea. My usually quiet voice came out strong as I stood–a testament in itself– and gave witness! Praising, I shouted, "All glory to God!" and my sisters repeated the same.

Although I knew it was God's power that healed me, I also believe that the intercession of St. Clare played a role.

Immediately before the retreat that week, I had attended a program on the mystic saints put on by Women of Grace's Benedicta Institute. Before leaving, we were invited to choose a small picture of one of the female mystic's we had studied to take home with us. I held Our Lady of

Sorrows in my hand, but eyed St. Clare on the table in front of me. *Ahh, there are extras*, I thought, and placed her in my bag. I had carried that picture with me throughout the retreat, and often gazed on it in prayer. I know that St. Francis's "Little Plant," as St. Clare referred to herself, was interceding for me all weekend.[1]

Without knowing it, in many ways my spiritual life has been shaped by the Franciscan charism shared by St. Francis and St. Clare. For example, in my youth, I sang and had particular love for the song based on the prayer of St. Francis of Assisi, "Make Me a Channel of Your Peace." I held those words in my heart throughout my life, seeing it as a beautiful way to live.

Later in life, I found the Eternal Word Television Network, created by the well-known Poor Clare nun Mother Angelica. I learned so much from her and from other EWTN hosts, including Johnnette Benkovic Williams, who had been invited to the network by Mother Angelica, where she started the apostolate Women of Grace. This spiritual apostolate for Catholic women is heavily influenced by the Carmelite charism, but as part of EWTN, it is still part of the fruit of St. Clare's branch of the vine.

Now a member of Women of Grace, I have grown in my faith and love the contemplative prayer life. Sharing time and experiences with women striving for holiness, by the grace of God, is a treasure, as members learn in humility to pray to Jesus through Mary.

So, I owed much of my formation to St. Clare and her modern-day followers. I began to see how she'd been present through the retreat, praying for me. No doubt she had been praying for me my whole life, from the moment my life began.

Before time began, God created us to be good and holy in his sight.[2] While Clare was in the womb, her mother asked God for protection over herself and her infant. She heard a voice say, "You will give birth to a light

---

1   Rejis J. Armstrong, OFM Cap., *Clare of Assisi – The Lady: Early Documents* (New York: New City Press, 2006), 67.

2   See Ephesians 1:3–4.

that will shine brightly in the world."[3] Though the young Clare tried to stay hidden, her light could not be shuttered from those who knew her. Ioanni di Ventura of Assisi, a house watchman for the family who saw her offerings of fasting, prayer, and giving to the poor, said, "It seemed from the very beginning she was inspired by the Holy Spirit."[4]

As a follower of St. Francis, Clare had a conversion into the life of simplicity, poverty, humility, and obedience. She was the first woman to follow Francis.[5] The daughter of noble parents, Clare was expected to marry, yet she turned down many suitors to become a bride of Christ,[6] despite her father's insistence that she marry someone suitable for the benefit of the family.[7]

At eighteen, Clare snuck out in the middle of the night to find Francis and his brothers. She chose the door with heavy barricades to escape from the darkness of the world into the new light of holy poverty. In the morning, neighbors were amazed she was able to get the door opened. Sister Cristiana, who had been in the house that night, stated, "Clare alone, with the help of Jesus Christ, removed the barricades and opened the door."[8]

Clare's family pursued and found her. By then, Francis had already cut her long beautiful locks, and she had put on the tapestry of holy poverty with a rope as a belt, binding her to a new life. One man, perhaps her brother, grabbed Clare, trying desperately to take her home. She grasped the altar rail, refuting her family's pleading. Clare stated she would only be the Bride of Jesus Christ whom she loved more than any suitor! Her veil came off during the calamity, showing her bobbed hair, and her family left.[9]

---

3   *Clare of Assisi*, 161.
4   Ibid. 195.
5   *Lives of Saints*, Fr. Jospeh Vann. ed. (New York: John J. Crawley & Co, 1954), 259–260.
6   *Clare of Assisi*, 193.
7   Ibid., 194–195.
8   Ibid., 185.
9   *Lives of Saints*, 260.

Clare's sister Agnes, just fourteen years old, joined her. Many other elite women left their worldly riches for the eternal prize. After that, the Poor Ladies became established in San Damiano, Assisi, Italy. Francis named Clare as Superior.[10]

Although Clare was adamantly strict with herself, she was charitable with her sisters.[11] She clearly lived the gospel passage, "Whoever would be great among you must be your servant."[12] A shining example, Clare didn't hesitate to take on the menial tasks. She showed kindness to the sick and took on more plentiful admonishments than that of her sisters.[13] It was only under obedience, at the command of St. Francis, that Clare acquiesced to eating a small portion of bread and drinking water on the three days of the week she had previously had nothing to eat or drink.[14]

Clare had a rich contemplative prayer life.[15] Along with her daily prayers with her sisters, including reading and singing the Psalms, Clare woke up to pray during the night. At midnight, she frequently woke her sisters to praise the Lord with her, using a bell or sign since she only used words to speak about Godly things.[16] (I wondered—was she the one who woke me in time for the healing service or to discover my own healing in time to thank God in prayer before the others awoke?)

Additionally, she was often found in prayer lying flatly upon the earth in prostration to our Lord.[17] Clare's devotion established a memorable example of praying unceasingly.

I believe many things helped Clare to grow in unity towards the will of the Father. She frequented the sacraments, and she both knew and lived her faith. She centered her life on Jesus, and followed the example

---

10 *Claire of Assisi*, 143–144, 303.
11 Ibid., 50, 187.
12 See Matthew 20:26.
13 *Clare of Assisi*, 168.
14 Ibid., 151.
15 Ibid., 163.
16 Ibid., 152.
17 Ibid., 146.

of Mary. Together, these practices made her prayers greatly effective. Out of her faith and love, the Lord granted her miracles.

Clare is perhaps best known for the miracle of the Eucharist against the Saracens, who were Islamic invaders. These mercenaries had terrorized, killed, and tortured sisters in other cities. They had their sights on San Damiano and were climbing ladders to enter the monastery. Clare, ill in bed, was awakened by her fellow sisters.[18]

Her thoughts were not of herself, but the others. She prayed, "I beseech thee, O Lord, protect those whom now I am not able to protect." The Lord answered, and all present heard, "I will have them always in my care."[19]

When the Saracens came over the walls, the sisters were in prayer with Clare, who held Jesus in the monstrance. When she raised the monstrance, the invading soldiers, who lived in the darkness of outrageous sins, couldn't stand the Light of the World and left without harming anyone.[20]

Clare also had a healing gift. One of her nuns, Sister Amato, had endured thirteen months of suffering due to dropsy, fever, and cough. After receiving a word from the Lord that her sister had endured enough, Clare made the Sign of the Cross on her sister's forehead. She was immediately healed.[21]

Many witnesses attested to the holiness of Clare as befitting a saint. The light of God was shown through her in miraculous ways, though in her humility she took no credit for it. Clare must have known, through living in Divine Providence, that none of it came from her own accord but from our Trinitarian God.

Perhaps even more than for my physical healing, I owe St. Clare gratitude for inspiring and healing me in spiritual matters. For example, as I reflect on her simple life, I realize how many times I have felt owned

---

18 Julie Onderko, *Holy Handmaids of the Lord* (Manchester, NH: Sophia Institute Press, 2019), 51.
19 *Clare of Assisi,* 174–175.
20 Ibid., 11, 159; see John 3:20.
21 Ibid., 163–164.

by my possessions. Clare's holy simplicity of living in the manner of Jesus, Mary, and St. Francis inspires me—and all of us—to look outside ourselves to the needs of others, rather than what the world can provide for us. In this way, freed from our attachment to possessions, God's light will shine through us as well.

But to live in this manner, I need to trust the Lord, just as I did with my healing. How? Again, Clare shows the way. I don't live in holy poverty within a convent like St Clare. However, I can follow her example through living a simple sacrificial life and allowing God, through His grace, to help me detach from the things of this world.

This doesn't always happen suddenly, as when St. Clare left the home of her parents. Rather, over time we learn how to sacrifice in love of God and neighbor and cling to His Divine Providence.

And over time, our prayers are answered and our suffering seen. I'm convinced St. Clare was interceding for me in compassion, knowing I had suffered these symptoms over thirty years.

Although I am still disabled, and I use a wheelchair for fatigue and distance, the symptoms of all-over muscle stiffness, painful pressure points, and burning trigger points are now totally gone! Although the doctors say this is due to medicine, that in itself is a gift from God. Nothing and no one can stop me from knowing that I went to sleep one way and woke up totally changed. I was able to stand straight and walk freely on a day I should have been totally fatigued and more than ready to go home. Many witnesses can attest to this. All Glory to God!

My heart believes that in my youth, as I turned to the prayer of St. Francis, St. Clare began her intercession for me. Her prayers allowed me to find Mother Angelica, who inspired me with her reliance on God to take care of everything.

She interceded for me in finding Women of Grace, where I learned feminine maternal spirituality, which is necessary for the salvation of all. It is through our wombs that God creates each of His children but also calls women to be spiritual mothers and bring them to the fullness of life.

No doubt It was St. Clare's compassion, one of her feminine qualities, that moved her to turn toward me in my suffering.

Clare's intense prayer life inspired me to join in prayer ministry through Women of Grace. I am filled with joy as I humbly pray online, as I am able, with other beautiful sisters at many different hours, for the reparation of sins and for holy intentions. Our prayers include the Flame of Love Rosary, Our Lady's Sorrows, and the Divine Mercy Chaplet, given to us through holy saints and mystics.

Therefore, turn to St. Clare when you need compassion, spiritual motherhood, and healing in any form. Suffering is suffering, and it comes in many ways, including wounds of the heart. You may not need relief from the kind of long physical suffering I endured, but no doubt you have need of some kind of healing. When we ask for St. Clare's intercession, we can rely on her in all matters small or great, and know with greater confidence that no matter how or when our prayers are answered, our sufferings and our healings are all for our good and God's glory. Perhaps this is St. Clare's greatest "light"—to shine upon God's Word and reveal that He brings all things together for good. May this bring you great hope through her intercession.

St. Clare, pray for us.

Prayer to St. Clare of Assisi

Ruth Ellen Naef

Beautiful light of compassion, shining with the Trinity,

*Pray that we may always be willing to sacrifice for
the Lord, trusting in His Divine Providence.*

*Help us to know the ways of the world are entrapments,
and the ways of God are freedom.*

*Help us to grow in unity with the Father,
His Divine Son, Jesus Christ and the Holy Spirit.*

*May we allow God to perfect us each day,
that our souls become pure and to shine like yours.*

*May we, by the grace and mercy of God, win the battle against
temptations of the devil and cling to Mary and Jesus.*

St. Clare, please intercede for all our needs.

Amen.

Knowing that we are called to an ongoing, deepening conversion, **Ruth Ellen Naef** believes that suffering can be an opportunity to grow in our relationship with God. Ruth Ellen is a wife of thirty-seven years and a mom of two. She is an active member of her parish, Women of Grace, and the PraiseWriters community. You can follow her at her website *Ruthellennaef.com*.

XXVI

A CALL TO HEAL

How St. Joseph Spiritually Adopted Me

Jonathan Cunningham

S ilence and stillness encapsulated the space in the crypt beneath the main sanctuary. Though pilgrims and tourists milled about, a certain peace permeated the air.

The sense of interior calm that I was experiencing was partially due to the fact that my sister, brother-in-law, and I were also staying a few nights at the retreat residence on the serene grounds of the St. Joseph's Oratory in Montreal, Quebec.

Just that morning, we had eaten a light breakfast on the elevated patio, taking in the cool breeze beneath the sturdy trees, as two squirrels danced and played on the railing, seeking a meal of their own. A variety of languages floated by from others' conversations, though the local French prevailed.

Later that day, we took a short hike up the steep hill, whose name means "Royal Mount," and made it to the grandiose Renaissance revival-style basilica shrine atop the outlook. With a feeling of being removed from the world, we entered below the grand external staircase and were surrounded by St. Joseph devotional statues.

Spending our time praying with tranquility in front of the various patronages, which lined the long hallway in flickering red and green candlelight, we offered our relevant intentions at each particular station.

Our pilgrimage ended at a memorial to St. André Bessette, which was surrounded by an exposed surface of the Mont Réal itself. This humble, holy man is responsible for spreading greater devotion to our adopted spiritual father. Many other saints have done similarly for this *protodulia*—the greatest of all saints after the Virgin Mary.

A number of months later, I began the *Consecration to St. Joseph*, compiled by Donald H. Calloway, MIC. This spiritual exercise gave me such a deeper awareness of the legacy of the adoptive father of our Lord, how he has continually shepherded the Church toward his adopted Son, and his ability to be a powerful intercessor for us all.

Through my own deepening devotion to St. Joseph, perhaps what has surprised me the most is St. Joseph's desire to spiritually adopt *me*—and all of us—into the Holy Family. My early childhood was impacted by a serious illness, which significantly affected my family's course. While I am extremely thankful for the support and stability of my family during that time and my preserved health since then, I have been reminded that—no matter our upbringing or life journey—we all have healing to do.

By allowing St. Joseph to spiritually adopt me, I have more readily received the reconciling graces of God's mercy to discover this restoration. In turn, I have tried to emulate the virtues of St. Joseph, and have found peace by offering myself to Jesus through St. Joseph.

+ + +

St. Joseph was raised in a faithful and fortunate family with a clear plan for life. He came from royal heritage and was a faithful Jew. He was engaged to an immaculate woman. However, his story was interrupted, as he was invited to participate in the story of salvation history.

Initially, the most holy marriage-to-be almost ended in a quiet divorce (though some note that St. Joseph intended to quietly separate from Mary because possibly he felt unworthy to invite into his home the woman he knew would bear the Son of God). Thankfully, as with other biblical figures, God sent an angel to clarify His plan, and due to St. Joseph's faith and fortitude, "when Joseph awoke, he did as the angel of the Lord commanded him and took his wife into his home" (Matthew 1:24).

Though he resolutely followed God's call, he initially had a period of doubt. As such, in whatever our vocational struggles, St. Joseph can accompany us and model for us how to follow God's call.

Soon, St. Joseph faced the reality of being an expectant father. After Mary conceived of the Holy Spirit, he faced the challenge of guarding and providing for his pregnant wife on their journey for the census, including the difficulty of finding there to be no room at an inn for the Virgin Mary to give birth.

Nonetheless, he continued to faithfully follow God's invitation to foster the Incarnation into the world. Likewise, wherever our lives lead, St. Joseph can show us how they can always be submitted to God's will and directed toward bearing Christ into the world.

One characteristic central to this theme is St. Joseph's silent patience. I find it interesting to reflect on the difference between the responses of the Virgin Mary and of St. Joseph to the angel's message. While Mary's beautiful Magnificat echoes throughout the ages of the Church, St. Joseph's fiat is hidden.

His firm faith and still solace is evident when he immediately chooses to take Mary into his home after receiving the angelic message in his dream. His actions required a certain silence to be able to hear God's voice and patience to resolve to follow it, even though he did not completely understand God's plan. Through his distinctive reticence, he portrays how interior stillness creates space for God to act in our lives and in the world.

In my own illness experience, I have often struggled with asking, *why me?* However, St. Joseph clearly exemplifies the way in which we should approach God in our uncertainty: by patiently bearing our sufferings, and experiencing God's faithfulness to us in them, we can form hope in the fact that God can bring good out of every situation.

Another relevant virtue is that of purity. St. Joseph particularly exemplifies this quality through his respect and care for the Virgin Mary. As a young man, his chastity allowed him to identify and turn away from the temptations of the flesh. Not only did he trust God's plan of bearing life within the Virgin Mary, but he also gave up his own physical desires for the greater glory of God. By sacrificing his will, God was able to sanctify his life (the word "sacrifice" coming from the Latin *sacra* "holy" + *facere* "to make").

Our culture has become littered with profanities disrespecting the human body. However, as St. John Paul II notes in his *Theology of the Body*, the marriage of the Virgin Mary and Joseph is the purest example of human love. Through studying these writings of the modern saint, I have seen how St. Joseph can help us to restore such purity in our society. When we surrender our desires to God for the good of others, we can imitate Joseph's purity of heart, and God can make our lives holy as well.

Following the Nativity, St. Joseph led the Holy Family through their flight to Egypt. He supported them in abject poverty and as uprooted migrants. As such, St. Joseph's heart is close to the poor and those without a home.

If the holiest of families were faced with scarcity and homelessness, imagine how much dignity they instill into the lives of those who similarly struggle today. Therefore, we should turn to St. Joseph to learn how to better embrace the poor and wayward, in whom we find images of the Holy Family.

This poverty necessitates a profound humility. In responding to the challenges of their lives, with limited resources and reserved lifestyles, St. Joseph displays how having such docility is the most important way to detach oneself from the world and to submit oneself to God's will.

Throughout the ages, saints with a devotion to St. Joseph have modeled a powerful humility and invite us to the same. For example, St. André Bessette emulated this poorness in spirit through his service of the needy and ill. Though he was a simple porter at a Canadian college, his life brought forth many miracles and began a movement of deeper devotion to St. Joseph.

+ + +

As Jesus grew in wisdom and age and favor, St. Joseph moved more into the background of the story of the Holy Family. He was still present, but with the ordinary repetition of daily life, he weaved himself into the Gospel narrative.

Joseph is the one who first instructed Jesus in the Jewish faith, in work, and in manhood. He also cared for Mary in her needs. Surely they would not have been the same without his diligent support.

His work must have taken on supernatural significance as he guided Jesus in crafting carpentry. Having the Son of God in his workshop, he must have been keenly aware of God's presence in his daily activities. Ultimately, it was through his constant reliance on God's grace and his diligent efforts to devote everything to Him that he was such an exceptional worker.

In my own occupation, I have taken inspiration from another devotee of St. Joseph—St. Josemaría Escrivá. Just as St. Joseph models for us, the founder of Opus Dei professes the universal call to holiness, primarily through the sanctification of work and an awareness of our divine affiliation. In imitation of these—and many other—great saints, we can strive to look to Jesus to direct our professional goals and to overcome sinful tendencies in the demands of our daily activities.

+ + +

Through his virtues of patience, purity, humility, and diligence, St. Joseph was a model father for the Holy Family. Similarly, he can be a spiritual father for us all.

If you have been blessed with a sturdy relationship with your father, thank God and ask St. Joseph to pray for continued blessings on him. However, many people have had imperfect childhoods, whether from external circumstances or uncontrollable traumas. Unfortunately, strong fathers are sometimes lacking in today's world.

In this paternal absence, we can allow ourselves to be adopted by St. Joseph into the Holy Family, to regain our sense of how we are ultimately invited into divine communion with the Holy Trinity. I have discovered a deep solace in prayerfully considering how Mary, Joseph, and Jesus are able to help restore and transform the memories of my own childhood challenges when I accept their offer of adoption.

By prayerfully reflecting on our lives, and seeking psychological support when necessary, we can come to heal from our past difficulties and learn how to approach our present with the awareness that the Holy Family is able to help us properly respond to the ongoing crosses that we carry.

+ + +

When St. Joseph takes us under his patronage, we are spiritually adopted into the Holy Family. Through this story, we not only carry the weight of our fallen ancestors, but we also gain the redemptive grace of having Jesus as our brother and the Virgin Mary and St. Joseph as our constant intercessors.

In the witness of St. Joseph, the necessity of trusting God's will, the value of marriage and the family, the dignity of the impoverished and homeless, and the sanctity of work are exemplified in his patience, purity, humility, and diligence. Ultimately, these aspects make him into an epitome of fatherhood. As our adopted spiritual father, we can go to him for guidance in how to grow in these qualities and how to share his adopted Son's message with the world.

In my own journey in coming to know St. Joseph more, I have seen how, though he may appear hidden, if we seek him out, he will readily guide us to his adopted Son. I would like to close with a poem that I recently wrote, in front of the St. Joseph side altar in St. Peter's Basilica, while on pilgrimage to Rome:

> *Adopted spiritual father,*
> *Teach me how to be*
> *A holy man of God:*
>
> *Patient, yet firm;*
> *Pure, yet passionate;*
> *Humble, yet unafraid;*
> *Diligent, yet understanding;*
>
> *When I rest, let me rise*
> *Ready to follow His call.*
>
> *When I work, let me rest*
> *In the peace of His providence.*
>
> *When I suffer, let me work*
> *For the salvation of souls.*
>
> *In the silence of your gaze,*
> *Adopted father of Jesus and us all,*
> *Let us foster Christ into the world*
> *As you did through surrendering*
> *To Him who makes all things new.*

Jonathan Cunningham believes that our lives are stories, and no matter the content, they can become meaningful. Through his blog *Do Not Conform; Be Transformed* and other projects, he explores ways to intentionally craft life narratives, primarily through strengthening our connection with God and others. Follow his story and download a printable morning prayer devotional at *theworldinverse.com.*

XXV

DO WHATEVER HE TELLS YOU

How Mary, Mother of Good Counsel, Helped Me Mother My Children with Trust

Carrie Sanchez

I knew I was in trouble.

As I was driving down the road, I glanced in the rearview mirror at my newborn baby peacefully sleeping in her carseat. My heart pounded at the reality of being a mother.

Panic swept over me. *I have a baby! I am responsible for this little soul. How on earth can this be? I have no idea what I am doing! How will I teach her everything she needs to know? How will I protect her from a world come undone? How will I know how to navigate all the complex issues of her innocent heart?*

The questions assaulted me for a mile, and then I felt a presence I couldn't articulate at the time. A deep peace settled over me, into my mind, body, and heart. Two phrases enveloped me. "Behold, I am the handmaid of the Lord; let it be to me according to your word" (Luke 1:38), and "Do whatever He tells you" (John 2:5). Mary's words, spoken into my heart in that moment, are alive today through Jesus's Eternal word. That day, her words began to take on new significance for me.

Our Blessed Mother, Mary, encompasses all that each of us were created to be, which is why I love praying the Litany of Loreto. Each name highlights her virtues and various roles as our Blessed Mother.

The Litany of Loreto was composed during the Middle Ages. The place of honor it now holds in the life of the Church is due to its faithful use at the shrine of the Holy House at Loreto. Pope Sixtus V definitively approved the litany in 1587, and all other Marian litanies were suppressed, at least for public use.[1]

All of the titles of Our Lady are meaningful to me—she has ministered to me in so many different ways throughout my life—but there is something striking and special about her name and role as Mary, Mother of Good Counsel, which was earned by Our Lady with her declaration at the Wedding Feast of Cana, "Do whatever He tells you" (John 2:5).

Driving down the road, as my racing heart began to slow to a manageable pace, I began pondering the peace that placated my panic just moments before. With that pondering came a gift in the form of a word of knowledge. I have prayed with this word ever since that day. The gift was wrapped in several truths that I slowly unwrapped on that drive home—and continue to unwrap eighteen years later.

The first layer was the invitation to trust that God created each one of us for a particular purpose and plan. The next layer: I do not have to invent my identity, I do not need to have all the answers, and I do not need to figure it all out. Rather, I simply need to trust that God is the Creator and will show and guide me every step of the way.

God does this in many ways but namely by giving us Mary as an example. When we emulate Mary, Mother of Good Counsel, especially her humility, listening, acting, and resolutely obeying her weighty words, "Do whatever He tells you," great fruit is born.

---

1 https://www.ewtn.com/catholicism/devotions/litany-of-loreto-246

My feminine genius and my mothering heart desire to love deeply. I desire to follow Mary's example of giving of herself fully, always acting in holy obedience ... but there's a small detail that complicates my situation.

I am not Mary.

Not even close. I was not given the gift of perfect grace at my conception. On my own, I fail greatly and often. Nevertheless, I have learned to praise God for this lack, because each day in my weakness, I can grow and learn how to die to self and lean into the divine assistance that is offered to all of us. I need a lot of help to navigate this world in general, and motherhood specifically, with grace and beauty. Mary's beautiful heart always provides her beloved children with good counsel; all we have to do is ask. She is not a figure of the past, but alive and present to us today in our everyday lives.

There are several powerful stories where Mary, Mother of Good Counsel, has so lovingly mothered me in the mothering of my children. She has counseled me when I just didn't know what to do. One such recent story illustrates not only how Mary has mothered me but also how she has helped mother my daughter.

My daughter, all bias aside, is elegantly beautiful. She stands dignified and regal, but at six feet tall, her teenage heart struggled with body image and being able to accept and feel comfortable in her own skin. She brought those concerns to the Lord during the National Eucharistic Congress held in Indianapolis in 2024.

Through many of the talks she attended, the Lord spoke to her about the beautiful way in which He created her. He imparted to her that He designed her perfectly to look the way that she does. He also wanted her to trust Him in this truth and invited her to praise Him with her whole mind, soul, and body. One of the speakers suggested that our bodies are an extension of our heart, so when we physically lift our hands to the Lord, it is like your heart is reaching out to Him too.

On the last evening of the Eucharistic Congress, my daughter knew she was being invited to acquiesce and trust the Lord with what He had been speaking to her all week. She decided to respond in trust. During the evening praise and worship music, she boldly raised her hands up high and began singing and praising with her whole mind, soul, and body.

Within seconds of doing so, she heard a hiss behind her spitting out words with a snide attitude. "A real Christian wouldn't block the view of someone behind them. Can you imagine being that tall!?"

Now the Lord knows exactly what we need at all moments. Providentially, I had not yet arrived back from the airport after dropping off my husband and other daughter to witness this event. If I had been there, you would have heard the clink of the steel of my mama bear claws coming out for attack. When I did arrive moments later, I watched my beautiful daughter turn around to a woman behind her and collapse crying into her arms. I knew something deep had transpired, but it was not the time nor the place to go into it. So we chose to be present in the moment and continued adoring and praising our Lord.

At the end of the night, my daughter shared with me all that happened. Right after hearing the hiss of the person speaking those words behind her, the first praise and worship segment ended. The next speaker opened with the St. Michael the Archangel prayer. My daughter sat in amusement with the Lord about that timing and moved down a seat so she was no longer in front of that woman.

Another praise and worship session began and another woman arrived and sat down directly behind my daughter. My daughter turned and asked the woman, newly seated behind her, if it was OK to stand to praise and worship during Adoration. All she said was "of course," in the most motherly way—so casual and warm and friendly, which is when my daughter fell into her arms crying. We continued singing and praising the Lord when the leaders announced Adoration would begin shortly. Jesus was processed out in the Monstrance, and the woman who had hissed the judgmental words departed.

At the end of the night, my daughter turned to the warm woman, thanked her again, and told her, "You'll never know how much that meant to me." The woman spoke life into my daughter saying, "You are going to do great things with your life, and this is just the beginning. Also, I don't know why, but I really feel like I'm supposed to give you this rosary bracelet." My daughter graciously accepted the generous gift and asked the lady's name.

Her name was Mary. *Do whatever He tells you.*

This isn't where the story ends. The next day, the Eucharistic Congress closed with Mass and a sending-forth message. Our drive home was quite long, so we stayed overnight on our trek back to Texas. Logically it would have made sense to go through St Louis, but I received a prompting of a different sort to go through Memphis. *Do whatever He tells you.*

We were driving two cars home—my boys and I were in one car, and my sister-in-law and daughter were in the other. I love how much the Lord knows us intimately. Even though my sister-in-law and I left the hotel in Memphis at the same time, I managed to ride on the wings of the speedy cars in front of me. God knew I would. I was about an hour ahead of the second car, so I was able to give my sister-in-law a heads-up that there was an upcoming slowdown. God, knowing her intimately, knew she would pull over immediately to fill up with gas as a precautionary measure. *Do whatever He tells you.*

Her heart quickened when she realized that she had pulled over in a less-than-ideal spot. The people milling about looked somewhat dangerous, and dilapidated buildings littered the landscape. She knew the environment was not safe for two young women. No faster than coming to that realization, my daughter saw a homeless woman and feverishly began gathering protein bars, a rosary, and prayer cards. *Do whatever He tells you.*

A fair amount of debate passed between my daughter and sister-in-law out of concern for safety, but the Lord provided a prudent way for my daughter to safely approach the woman. My daughter asked her name, which was Christy. This woman shared her sacred story, ending with the words, "I have no family, no home, and I don't know what to do." My daughter prayed with her, spoke life into her, gave her a rosary, protein bars, and her phone number. *Do whatever He tells you.*

In the communications that ensued afterwards, my daughter was able to put her in touch with Catholic Charities and eventually also with a group that was able to care for her temporal needs. My daughter and Christy continued texting over the next few weeks and months offering prayers and consolations to one another. Christy told her she had started attending a nearby church and also received devastating news of a cancer diagnosis. Upon hearing that news, my daughter went to Adoration, praying and crying out to the Lord on her behalf. The following week, on the morning of Our Lady's birthday, my daughter received a text from Christy with the words, "I am getting baptized today!" *Do whatever He tells you.*

This once peacefully sleeping baby in the rearview, now a beautiful young person witnessing the good news of the Gospel, is a testimony to the power and virtue of entrusting ourselves to Mary, Mother of Good Counsel's loving heart and guidance.

We have a loving Father, a blessed Mother, and an entire cloud of witnesses interceding on our behalf. They are running alongside us, cheering, consoling, and offering good counsel on our incredible journey, answering our universal call to holiness. Thank you, Mary, Mother of Good Counsel, for bestowing your wisdom and mother's heart to me and all that ask for your intercession in our everyday lives. May we all, like you, do whatever He tells us.

Carrie Sanchez is a singer, speaker, writer, wife, and mother that loves sharing stories to help bridge the gap between theology and our everyday lives. Come share your story with her at *carriesanchez.net.*